"Brother Andrew lived by a simple but potent creed: If you fear God, you need not fear any man. While I'm sad this is his last book now that the Lord has taken him home to glory, I'm so grateful this dear Dutch brother—and his steadfast colleague Al Janssen—wrote *Fearless by Faith* before it was too late. It's an absolute gem. Encouraging. Inspiring. And so timely. As the world seems to spin wildly out of control and persecution against the Church intensifies, we urgently need to discover the lessons that Brother Andrew gleaned from the Scriptures, truths that gave him great courage to take the light of Christ into great darkness. I've learned so much from the biblical prophets and warriors that Brother Andrew studied and taught about—David, Elijah, Jonah, Moses and Gideon. I pray you will, too."

Joel C. Rosenberg, *New York Times* bestselling author
of such titles as *The Last Jihad*, *Epicenter*
and *Enemies and Allies*

"*Fearless by Faith* is a book I wish I could have read as a new believer at age eighteen. The Bible-centered life of Brother Andrew plus the writing skills of Al Janssen masterfully center modern spiritual challenges squarely within the Word of God. My mentor reminded me endlessly, 'Whenever you have a spiritual problem you cannot solve, what Bible story are you telling yourself that addresses your challenge?' Brother Andrew and Al Janssen prophetically present us with a Bible that is in active present tense! Andrew believed the Bible was not only a record of what God used to do but a clear spiritual road map illuminating God's demands upon His children. What a gift!"

Dr. Nik Ripken, founder and CEO, Nik Ripken Ministries

Fearless
by FAITH

Fearless by FAITH

HOW *to* FIGHT
TODAY'S SPIRITUAL BATTLES

BROTHER ANDREW and AL JANSSEN

Chosen

a division of Baker Publishing Group
Minneapolis, Minnesota

© 2023 by Open Doors International

Published by Chosen Books
Minneapolis, Minnesota
www.chosenbooks.com

Chosen Books is a division of
Baker Publishing Group, Grand Rapids, Michigan

Printed in the United States of America

All rights reserved. No part of this publication may be reproduced, stored in a retrieval system, or transmitted in any form or by any means—for example, electronic, photocopy, recording—without the prior written permission of the publisher. The only exception is brief quotations in printed reviews.

ISBN 978-0-8007-6320-6 (cloth)
ISBN 978-1-4934-4102-0 (ebook)

Library of Congress Cataloging-in-Publication Control Number: 2022053375

Unless otherwise indicated, Scripture quotations are from The Holy Bible, English Standard Version® (ESV®), copyright © 2001 by Crossway, a publishing ministry of Good News Publishers. Used by permission. All rights reserved. ESV Text Edition: 2016

Scripture quotations identified MSG are taken from *THE MESSAGE*, copyright © 1993, 2002, 2018 by Eugene H. Peterson. Used by permission of NavPress. All rights reserved. Represented by Tyndale House Publishers, Inc.

Scripture quotations identified NASB taken from the (NASB®) New American Standard Bible®, Copyright © 1960, 1971, 1977, 1995, 2020 by The Lockman Foundation. Used by permission. All rights reserved. www.lockman.org

Scripture quotations identified NIV are from THE HOLY BIBLE, NEW INTERNATIONAL VERSION®, NIV® Copyright

© 1973, 1978, 1984, 2011 by Biblica, Inc.® Used by permission. All rights reserved worldwide.

Scripture quotations identified NLT are taken from the Holy Bible, New Living Translation, copyright © 1996, 2004, 2015 by Tyndale House Foundation. Used by permission of Tyndale House Publishers, Inc., Carol Stream, Illinois 60188. All rights reserved.

Scripture quotations identified TLB are from The Living Bible, copyright © 1971. Used by permission of Tyndale House Publishers, Inc., Carol Stream, Illinois 60188. All rights reserved.

Cover design by Studio Gearbox

Published in association with Yates & Yates, www.yates2.com

Baker Publishing Group publications use paper produced from sustainable forestry practices and post-consumer waste whenever possible.

23   24   25   26   27   28   29   7   6   5   4   3   2   1

To God's Smugglers

Thousands of faithful couriers who followed Brother
Andrew's example and challenge by passing through the
Iron Curtain to deliver desperately needed Bibles and other
printed resources to our Christian brothers and sisters
in Communist Eastern Europe and the Soviet Union.

Contents

Contents

When you fear God, you fear nothing else.

Oswald Chambers,
The Pilgrim's Song Book

Life without war is impossible in the natural
or the supernatural realm. It is a fact that
there is a continuing struggle in the physical, mental, moral, and spiritual areas of life.

Oswald Chambers,
My Utmost for His Highest

Preface

Brother Andrew was a warrior who was eager to rush in where others feared to go. When the Soviet Union invaded Czechoslovakia in 1968, he loaded his station wagon with Bibles and drove 550 miles from his home in the Netherlands. As he pulled up to the Czech border, a long line of cars was departing the country. A shocked customs official stamped his passport and waved him through the gate. In Prague, he armed Christians with Russian Bibles and told them to go into the streets, climb on the tanks, tell the invaders that God loves them and hand them God's Word.

That is how you dismantle a superpower—with love, not bombs.

As Communism in the Soviet empire collapsed, Brother Andrew turned his attention to radical Islam. He made friends with leaders of Hamas and Hezbollah so they could hear the

Gospel. He invited himself to one of the world's most radical madrassas, observed hundreds of boys memorizing the Quran and arranged for them to hear a better, greater message. The school's founder and principal watched and listened in amazement, seemingly powerless to stop this Christian invader.

These stories might imply that the Dutchman known as "God's Smuggler" was unique in that he did not experience fear. Not so. His secret was that he knew how to overcome his anxiety. Approaching the Iron Curtain with a car that was loaded with hundreds of Bibles, he sometimes had to pull back and spend a day or two in prayer and fasting before he had faith to proceed. He said the secret was, "If you fear God, you need not fear any man." Brother Andrew was not fearless, but he learned how to *fear less.*

Why are most of us afraid to confidently live out our faith? I ask that question every time I get another email from a friend who is worrying about his or her First Amendment rights, the advancement of certain political ideologies or how the election of certain leaders proclaims the doom of our nation. The COVID-19 pandemic seems to have raised the decibel level of alarm. Instead of loving behavior, too many Christians bicker about wearing masks and shout at one another about whether or not to vaccinate.

Make no mistake, fear is natural when battles rage all around. The antidote is supernatural. Scripture tells us that our earthly struggles are located in heavenly places (see Ephesians 6:12). In the midst of all the clamor, one thing seems to be forgotten. There is an author of all this confusion. He is God's sworn enemy, and he brilliantly sows fear in our ranks. The Church needs to awaken to the real battle that occurs in the spiritual realm and spills into every conflict on planet earth.

God invites us to partner with Him in that struggle. To do that, we must overcome our fears. I had the privilege of working and traveling with Brother Andrew for twenty years. With typical Dutch bluntness, he often made statements to me like this: "I think we in the West—this is a personal confession— are cowards. Personal profit comes first. If that is at risk, we don't do anything." He referenced fellow countrymen who refused to stand against the German occupation and the deportation of Jews during World War II. "There were ten times as many people in Holland in the armed SS as there were in the resistance movement." He often challenged Christians around the world to become "people of guts. And courage. And strong convictions. Not counting our lives dear unto ourselves if only we can fulfill the high calling of God in our lives."

That is what this book is about. *Fearless by Faith* contains Brother Andrew's teaching over many years on spiritual conflict, drawing from the examples of five Old Testament figures. Jesus promised that each of His followers would experience trouble in this world. We most certainly do! Jesus also encouraged us, "Take heart; I have overcome the world" (John 16:33). That is a tremendous reason why we should not be afraid. Or fear less. Maybe we know that in theory, but in the midst of our reality, it does not seem to help much. God's sworn enemy does everything in his power to blind us and thwart God's plan for our lives.

This devotional is designed to provide an antidote to fear. David, Elijah, Jonah, Moses and Gideon are going to teach us the essentials of spiritual warfare and demonstrate how to fight and prevail. The apostle Paul encourages us to learn from these great men. "For whatever was written in former days was written for our instruction, that through endurance and through the encouragement of the Scriptures we might have hope" (Romans 15:4).

What can these trainers who lived some three thousand years ago possibly teach us today when we have such advanced knowledge and technology at our fingertips? Let's start with this observation: God placed these people in impossible situations. They were doomed to fail unless . . . unless God showed up and did the miraculous. We do not like that. We would much prefer to have the world's best resources in our hands when we face opposition. God may use worldly tools, but His methods are definitely otherworldly.

You will be surprised how relevant our five Old Testament teachers are. Sure, God called them to unique assignments—I doubt many of us will be called to lead two million people out of slavery, to preach to a huge major metropolis or to challenge an entire pagan culture to a duel. But you never know. Dig deeper and you will find that each of these warriors might truly understand our challenges today.

While there is much these men can teach us, we need to listen for how the Holy Spirit would have us apply these lessons in our current circumstances and culture. We recommend, therefore, that you take your time reading through these teachings. Each devotional is short. You might choose to tackle just one per day. Take time to reflect and pray over the questions at the end of each reading.

The book is divided into two parts. The first part focuses on how we listen for God's instructions. Each warrior will provide six lessons. Part two concentrates on the spiritual battle. Again, each warrior provides six lessons. There will also be opportunities for you to articulate your own battle plan as you discern how God is uniquely calling you. Our fears are greatly diminished or even eliminated when we know what God has called us to do and understand that our conflicts belong to the Lord.

Al Janssen

Meet Your Instructors

David: A Rosy-Cheeked Warrior

We know the story. We learned it in Sunday school and enjoyed hearing it read from picture storybooks. It is the inspirational metaphor for the underdog sports team facing an undefeated opponent. It is the motivation for a startup company competing against a corporate giant.

Why revisit such a familiar drama as David and Goliath? Because when we stop and look closely, there are some things about this story that are relevant to fear and the spiritual warfare we experience today.

It is interesting how the two armies—Israel and the Philistines—are positioned for battle, yet no one lifts a sword. Not a single spear is thrown. No one is killed. There is just a lot of trash talk! Sounds like a big football match. Or election coverage in the media.

Here is the matchup. On one side stands a giant, a massively trained warrior. He is undefeated, impregnable and overconfident, and he issues the challenge: Send me your best man. We will fight. The loser serves the winner. No need for all of you to die in battle. Is it not better for one man to die for all?

Sounds reasonable, don't you think?

Meet our other contestant. No, not David. It is King Saul, the tallest man in all Israel. A trained soldier who is also undefeated. Saul versus Goliath. This is the match everyone anticipated. Saul's entire life had prepared him for this defining moment.

So where is Saul? Hiding in his tent. He is afraid. He has no intention of fighting the giant. (Neither did David, by the way. He came to the scene on an errand for his father, Jesse.) Saul knew he could not win. No doubt he prayed for someone to save him—anybody but him. He would write a check for half his personal wealth to the one who killed the giant. He would give his prettiest daughter in marriage to the champion. What other incentive could he provide? Okay, no taxes for the winner's entire family for life. Surely those were enough inducements to recruit a champion.

No one, however, stepped forward: For forty days. Until a teenage boy showed up.

So that is the situation. You know the ending. This story has been told and retold until there is no surprise left. Yet we should be surprised, amazed even, at what happened on that battlefield. Maybe David can show us how to confront and defeat the giants that we face. Consider this: David saw what everyone saw. David heard what everyone heard; however, David thought what no one thought. As a result, David said what no one said, and he did what no one did.

Are we going to cower in fear like Saul? Or will we step forward and trust God like the teenage shepherd? Before you start the devotions, read the full story in 1 Samuel 17.

Elijah: A Radical Warrior

This was the ultimate mismatch. Las Vegas would never post odds on this "contest." Four hundred and fifty prophets of Baal on one side. One lonely and reckless prophet of God on the other.

What was Elijah thinking? He could not have dreamed up such a contest—unless he had been divinely inspired.

Undoubtedly you recall the basics of this story. Elijah called for this match between the pagan god Baal and the Lord God of Israel on Mount Carmel. You also know the dramatic result. You may also think that it has little or no relevance to our world today. Actually, this drama has tremendous significance.

Consider, for example, the devastating implications of climate change. Elijah proclaims God's judgment: There will be no rain. Who controls the rain? This was Elijah's challenge to Israel. Are you going to place your trust in Yahweh, God, or the local counterfeit deity?

That should give us pause as we see the earth's temperature rising and the resulting increased ferocity of storms and fires raging through our forests. Where will we find the wisdom that we need to solve this problem?

Here is a bigger question: How can we deliver the Gospel to a hostile culture and radical extremists of various stripes without giving offense? Quick answer: We cannot. We live in trying times, and Christians must rise to the challenge. All of us need a large portion of Elijah in our lives. His story is extremely relevant to our present world situation.

We are going to examine how one great spiritual warrior fought a war—and won against impossible odds. To obtain the most from these teachings on Elijah, first read 1 Kings 17–19.

Jonah: A Rebellious Warrior

Jonah had a problem. He could not in good conscience obey God's command.

To understand Jonah's struggle, it might help to frame his mission in a contemporary context. "Jonah, arise and go to Mosul. Go to ISIS and preach to them, because their wickedness has come up before me."

God told Jonah to go to Nineveh, which was a town that was located in what today is northern Iraq, within the suburbs of Mosul. The Assyrians who lived in that great city were the most feared terrorists of that day. They hated Israel. They were making raids into the northern part of the country. Put it that way and perhaps we gain some sympathy for Jonah. We might have run away from that assignment, too.

As we study this short book, we will see just how relevant this drama is to our spiritual battles. Like Jonah, God has issued a call on our lives. Are we listening? Are we willing to go wherever He sends us in obedience? Or are we going to run away and spend our hard-earned money on a Mediterranean cruise?

We like quick solutions. We prefer short-term missions rather than a longtime commitment. Better yet, we prefer to do missions from a safe distance. Let's use smart bombs like Facebook or Twitter that can reach any target—except the hearts and minds of men. But it is hearts and minds we must touch if we are to have any chance of winning this spiritual war.

Take some time to read the four short chapters of the book of Jonah. Our twelve devotions are full of challenging questions that force us to make hard choices. The consequences of our choices could affect the future of our world.

Moses: A Retired Warrior

The history of Israel hinges on one old man who was retired from public service. Or so he thought.

The circumstances were dire. Injustice was rampant. There was forced labor, unfair working conditions, police brutality and ethnic cleansing. No question, the Israelites were in desperate straits. Protests were brutally suppressed. The people desperately needed a hero, someone who could stand up against the cruel system that had crushed the spirits of these people for hundreds of years.

The man God chose for this mission was eighty years old. He was ready to relax and enjoy the grandkids. At one time, he had held a prestigious position. But that was ancient history.

There would be no nation of Israel without Moses. His faith, his resolve, his courage, and most significantly, his prayers made all the difference. In the process, he came to know God more intimately than anyone else in the Old Testament.

The determination of Moses is astonishing. He was so compelled to intercede for the Israelites that he fasted for forty days, not once but twice, with hardly a break in between. It nearly killed him, but he did not care. He would pay any price to achieve the salvation of his people.

That is why the writer of the epistle to the Hebrews could say that Moses thought it was better to suffer for the sake of Christ than to own the treasures of Egypt (see Hebrews 11:26). Moses did not know Christ, yet he embodied the spirit of our Savior. Jesus even insisted to the Jewish religious leaders that Moses wrote about Him. "There is one who accuses you: Moses, on whom you have set your hope. For if you believed Moses, you would believe me; for he wrote of me" (John 5:45–46). If Jesus lifts Moses up for our edification, we must examine his life.

Our study covers a lot of ground. For part one, read Exodus 2–4. For part two, you will want to read Exodus 5–7, 14 and 32–34.

You probably think you cannot possibly live up to the example of Moses. Do not be so sure. God loves inserting people into impossible situations, regardless of their age or circumstance. The higher the stakes, the more we see His involvement, and the more we learn what He is like.

At the very least, you can be a prayer warrior, which may be the most significant job of your life. Moses will show you why and how.

Gideon: A Reluctant Warrior

There is no cookie cutter recruit for God's warriors. Sure, God uses similar spiritual practices to train us. But each person and each assignment is unique. You may be involved in a culture war or fighting social injustice—like Elijah or Moses. You could also be in some hidden or supportive role. Some of God's most important and effective soldiers are His intercessors. God invites us to influence our community, our nation and the world. We can literally direct history while we are on our knees.

There comes a time, however, when we are called to get off our knees and take action. Too many Christians say, "God has not called me." I would suggest that they have never listened for the call. Effective intercessors not only plead for people, but they listen for the heart of God. There likely will be a day when God invites you to be the answer to one or more of your prayers. So do not miss this critical point. Anyone can be a warrior in God's army.

Who, me?

Yes, you!

How do I know this? Because the last warrior who will train us was the least of the least, and he knew it. When Gideon was called by God to save Israel, he rightly noted that his clan was weakest in the half tribe of Manasseh, and he was the lowest in his father's household. He was a nobody. He had no standing in his community, much less in his nation. Only God saw his potential.

So, meet Gideon, a very ordinary person who was called by God to do an impossible job. His story is recorded in Judges 6–8. This conflict is another mismatch. Gideon's special forces were not the Navy SEALs or the Army's Green Berets. They could never have bested the massive Midianite army without supernatural help.

PART ONE

Fearless
LISTENING

Introduction

There is a postcard in my office that reads, "Good morning, God. What are You up to today? I want to be a part of it. May I? Thank You, Amen." That childlike prayer expresses my heart's desire.

The danger for too many Christians is that we would rather go to war for God than wait before Him and let His Spirit reveal to us what to do.

We face an enemy that wants to destroy the Body of Christ. Earth is the only place where the devil can have his way. Not in heaven—he has been thrown out. Our prayer life is the first part of dismantling enemy powers that want to overthrow the Kingdom of God.

Knowingly or unknowingly, willingly or unwillingly, we are either victims of the devil's power or we are the subjects of the love of God. If we are subjects of the love of God, we are filled with compassion, power and faith toward those who are caus-ing the war, those who oppose the Gospel of Jesus Christ. The conflict *must* begin with prayer. Pray for those who oppose or persecute you. That is what Jesus said (see Matthew 5:44).

Why do so many Christians wonder about God's will for their lives? Perhaps it is because we do not take the time to really listen for His instructions. There is so much noise in our world today, and so many demands, controversies and conflicts that compete for our attention. We see a need and decide we must act now.

But not every need is a call. If we try to fight too many battles, or the wrong battles, we will probably win none and wind up burned out—not to mention more anxious and fear-ful than ever.

The first step in dealing with fear is to gain God's perspec-tive. To do that, we must create space where we can hear Him speak. In this secret place, we take the first steps to victory. Each of our five Old Testament warriors learned that lesson. Let's take some time to reflect on how these men of God heard the Word of God. In the process, expect God to speak to *you*.

1

A Most Intimidating
Opponent

There came out from the camp of the Philistines a champion
named Goliath of Gath.

1 Samuel 17:4

Look at him! This Philistine warrior:

- is nearly ten feet tall
- wears 125 pounds of armor
- wields a spear that looks like a fence rail with a spear
  tip weighing 15 pounds
- carries a bronze sword

Goliath is a terrifying sight. That is the way it is with giants. They want you to believe your eyes and ears. They want you to recognize the impossible odds. Why fight when you know you cannot win? But if all you do is rely on your physical senses, you miss the full picture.

The apostle Paul understood the real enemy, and he taught that we are not fighting against the giants we see, but we are fighting the single giant we do not see (see 2 Corinthians 10:3–5). Our true enemy is the deceiver, the one who inspires every argument and lofty opinion raised up against the knowledge of God.

No doubt you will protest that Goliath was a real flesh and blood threat to Israel. Today a Christian suffering in persecution feels real pain, prejudice and rejection. Real flames burn their churches and homes. Inflexible iron bars enclose them in very real prisons. For some today the end is a martyr's death that leaves behind the agony of a grieving spouse, parent or pastor. These are realities we cannot ignore.

If the real enemy is unseen, then what exactly is going on in the Valley of Elah? As long as we view any Bible story as an isolated incident, we can never gain insight into the real battle. Everything in Scripture is recorded to teach us the character of God, the nature of spiritual warfare and the way of salvation.

The ultimate spiritual battle began early in Genesis when the serpent (our enemy, the devil) tempted Adam and Eve, and they ate the forbidden fruit. The devil told the first couple that they would now know good and evil. That seemed so attractive. He did not explain they would not have the power to do good nor would they have the power not to do evil.

God declared judgment on the devil. "I will put enmity between you and the woman, and between your offspring and her offspring; he shall bruise your head, and you shall bruise his heel" (Genesis 3:15). Here is the key to understanding all that follows in the Old Testament. The devil's objective is to prevent the promised offspring, the Redeemer, from being born. If he can do that, he wins and can continue to rule over planet earth.

Listen to David shouting after he heard Goliath's taunts. "Who is this uncircumcised Philistine?" (1 Samuel 17:26). The question implies the answer. Goliath is a heathen. He has no part of the Kingdom of God. He is an instrument of the devil whose purpose is to subvert the human race and make the birth of Messiah impossible. If Goliath wins this battle, the genealogy of David is broken and Satan thwarts God's plan.

Perhaps you think it is a different story today. Christ has come. He has redeemed us. He has established His Kingdom; however, the devil's rebellion persists. He continues to try to thwart the advancement of God's Kingdom throughout the world. He works constantly to prevent the return of Jesus so that He can claim what is rightfully His.

Do you recognize the spiritual warfare? The evidence is all around you. Just watch the news—you will see.

The devil has lost but he is not dead. He continues to take casualties.

Here is the point: A teenager filled with the Holy Spirit is more powerful than a monarch (Saul) God has abandoned. Unfortunately, Israel chose to trust in politics and found itself hopelessly adrift. When they were lined up against a super-power, they had no hope of victory. Is the situation any better today? Are not too many of us putting our hope in political so-lutions? We look to new laws, court decisions and charismatic leaders who shout simplistic promises over and over. Then we are disappointed when we do not get the expected results.

Do not worry. There *is* an answer. Those who understand the problem can make a difference. If you understand God's ways, *you* can be God's instrument to change the odds.

For Reflection

What evidence do you see of Satan's rebellion today? How is he trying to thwart the advancement of God's Kingdom?

2

Total Brainwashing

He stood and shouted to the ranks of Israel, ". . . I defy the ranks of Israel this day. Give me a man, that we may fight together."

1 Samuel 17:8–10

For forty days the Philistine came forward and took his stand, morning and evening.

1 Samuel 17:16

The giant does not bother to use his superior weaponry. Instead, he shouts. He uses words to intimidate Israel. It works. Israel listens to the lies, lies that are mixed with a little truth. This is a most effective tool of our enemy.

Listen to Goliath's taunt. "Why have you come out to draw up for battle?" (verse 8). This is a lie! Israel did not come out to make war against the Philistines. The Philistines invaded Israel. They occupied places where they did not belong. Goliath proposed a solution to the problem the Philistines caused.

The Philistines are engaged in psychological warfare. Day after day, week after week, Goliath repeats one message. Eighty times! Let's call this what it really is: brainwashing. Over and over the enemy shouts:

- You are slaves.
- You are powerless.
- If you try to fight me, I will crush you.
- You will never be free.
- You will always be weak.
- You will never have any weapons.
- You are worthless.
- You call yourselves people of God—how pathetic!

The Philistines do not have to fight. They do not need to take any risks. They have already won the battle of words. It is a rout: eighty to nothing.

When we look around the world, we are afraid of weapons of mass destruction. Certainly, various countries and terrorist groups pose serious threats; however, we really ought to be scared of something more powerful than any jihadist movement or emerging nuclear power. I am talking about *word* weapons. Jesus said, "Do not fear those who kill the body but cannot kill the soul" (Matthew 10:28). Atom bombs can kill only the body. Words destroy people's minds.

Our world is filled with destructive messages. Ideologies like Communism and Islamic fundamentalism claim millions. Philosophies embedded in many university courses try to capture our young people. Twenty-four hours a day the news media spouts words, words, words! And the people of God say almost nothing. We are so intimidated.

How many Christians believe these lies? We hear: You are powerless. You can never cope with your problems. You cannot change. You will never have victory over sin, so give up. You will never live the life God wants you to live.

Let's admit it: We are brainwashed. But there is a solution. We must fight these words with the Word. David knew and used the Word. The problem is that we do not know Scripture.

Ask Christians individually what their message is for the world today and many will admit they have no message. If we have not read our Bibles, then no wonder we are ignorant. Do you have a message? Every Christian, without exception, should have a message. The apostle Paul tells us to take up "the sword of the Spirit, which is the word of God" (Ephesians 6:17).

God's Word is infinitely superior to the giant's word! The enemy does not want you to have the Word. But why should he tell you what to read and what to believe?

The issue here is the power of God. We read that Jesus will hand over the Kingdom of God to His Father (see 1 Corinthians 15:24). This is the culmination of the spiritual battle. All power will belong to God. He will reign over all creation. This is what the devil is determined to prevent.

When I hear governments declaring that the Bible is a forbidden book, I rebel. That is never the will of God. When Communist countries decided they would determine how many Bibles, if any, were available for Christians, I refused to accept their declarations. I became "God's Smuggler." I believed, and still believe, that every Christian has a basic human right to read a copy of the Bible in his or her own language.

In many Muslim countries the situation is even worse than it was in Communist countries. It is harder to get Bibles into Saudi Arabia today than it was to get them into Russia in the 1960s. What are we going to do about this? We must not allow any religion or government to limit or regulate access to God's Word.

For Reflection

What evidence do you see today that words are brainwashing people's minds? Are you listening to the enemy's brainwashing or are you feeding on the Word of God? What is your plan for reading the Bible? Using Scripture, how can you resist Satan's messages?

3

Prepare to Be God's Answer

> The LORD said to Samuel, "How long will you grieve over
> Saul, since I have rejected him from being king over Israel? Fill
> your horn with oil, and go. I will send you to Jesse the Bethle-
> hemite, for I have provided for myself a king among his sons."
>
> 1 Samuel 16:1

Are you prepared for God to answer your prayers?

Here is a tougher question: Are you prepared to *be* God's answer to your prayers?

Despite his age, Samuel had to come out of retirement. For decades he had faithfully served the nation as a priest, a prophet and a judge. God gave the prophet one more assignment. He told him to stop grieving, to get up and to go! God had work for him to do.

There comes a time when prayer moves into action. Sometimes that takes years. Samuel did not give up praying for Saul and praying for the nation. But Samuel did not just pray; he was ready to be God's instrument to rescue the nation.

You may be thinking, *I can't slay giants in this world. I'm not a David. I'm too old (or too young). I'm not qualified. I'm weak. I've done all I can. I'm* _____. Fill in the blank. But there is something you *can* do. You can pray! Young or old, rich or poor, weak or strong, all of us have a responsibility to pray.

There are plenty of problems facing the world today. We can worry about them. We can talk about them. We can protest in the streets. We can form organizations that pressure politicians to solve them. We can give money. We can write blogs. The one thing we *must* do is pray. If Samuel does not pray, David is never identified as the solution to Israel's problem. Do you see the connection?

Are you frustrated with your nation's chief executive? Pray.

Are you fearful concerning your city's poverty or crime sprees? Pray.

Are you worried about your nation's moral fiber? Pray.

Are you fretting about your children and their walk with God? Pray.

Pray and listen. The two go together. Then be ready to act— not to rush out and solve the problem yourself.

King Saul would not wait when facing the Philistines in another battle (see 1 Samuel 13). The Philistines were about to attack, and Israel's army had scattered to the hills. Only a few hundred soldiers remained, and Saul had no idea how long they would stay with him. Before the battle was to begin, Samuel was to offer a sacrifice. When the prophet did not show up at the appointed time, Saul felt he had to act, and he did a stupid thing. He offered the sacrifice. God's instructions were clear—the priest, in this case Samuel, must perform the sacrifice. Saul needed to wait.

Saul disobeyed because it was the "logical" thing to do. When Samuel finally showed up, all he could do was proclaim God's verdict. Saul was foolish. Stupid! Saul, if only you had obeyed, God "would have established your kingdom over Israel for all time. But now your kingdom will not endure" (1 Samuel 13:13–14 NIV).

Pray. Wait patiently. And be prepared to move when God speaks.

Samuel thought his work was finished. He was retired. Still he prayed. God answered his prayers by giving him one final assignment. "Get up and go to Jesse of Bethlehem. I have chosen one of his sons to be king" (see 1 Samuel 16:1).

Samuel was not sure he had heard right. "I can't do that! If Saul hears about it, he will kill me," he protested.

God said, in essence, "Don't argue with Me. Just go and do it."

So, Samuel did as the Lord instructed him.

41

Meanwhile, David did not know it yet, but it was time to move from the sheep field to the battlefield. One day, not just any random day, Jesse gave David an assignment. (Who planted the thought in Jesse's mind?) Perhaps David arose that morning with nary an inkling that his life was about to change dramatically. He intended to go about his normal routine when Papa called him. "Take this grain and ten loaves of bread to your brothers. Also take these ten cheeses to their commander. See how your brothers are getting along and bring word back to me" (see 1 Samuel 17:17–18).

Obedience to God—what an exciting way to live! You never know what will happen next. When you least expect it, God may bring you face-to-face with a giant He intends for you to kill. You cannot possibly do it, of course.

For Reflection

What are you praying most about right now?
How will you know if and when God wants you
to be a part of His answer to your prayers?

4

Introducing the Man of God

The LORD has sought out a man after his own heart.
1 Samuel 13:14

Now David was the son of . . . Jesse, who had eight sons.
1 Samuel 17:12

It is tempting to think that David was mighty brave to step forward and confront Goliath. I do not believe that explains our hero. There were other brave men who could have fought the giant. Bravery alone does not ensure victory.

Where does God's person come from? It is hard to draw conclusions from David's background. When David was born, Saul had already been king for several years. David was the son of Jesse, an Ephrathite of Bethlehem. There were seven older brothers. I cannot help but wonder if David was a surprise child. Unexpected? Maybe. Unwanted? We do not know. From the family's actions, he appears to have been an afterthought.

One thing we do know—David was a boy after God's heart. Samuel told Saul that God was looking for such a person. Was David conscious that he was a man after God's heart? I kind of doubt it. But God recognized it.

How did David's spiritual journey begin? Maybe it began during a trip to the tabernacle. Or maybe it was due to Jesse's influence. Perhaps the love of his mother influenced him—it is interesting that absolutely no mention is made of her.

The songs David wrote reveal his heart for God, but they do not reveal how he began his spiritual journey. Did it start with a dream? Or the witness of a neighbor? Perhaps the seed was planted when Jesse's family celebrated Passover. David would have heard the story of Moses rescuing the Israelites from slavery and leading them across the Red Sea.

Maybe David's heart was kindled with love for God when he gazed at the stars one clear night as the sheep slept in the wilderness. "The heavens declare the glory of God, and the sky above proclaims his handiwork" (Psalm 19:1). So perhaps God's creation spoke to David and opened his spirit. Whatever the source, David acted on the light he saw. That was more than could be said for the priests and Levites who should have known the Law of Moses. Or for the royal court that had heard Samuel's instructions when King Saul was inaugurated.

One thing we do see of David is that he was a man of principle. David's character was evident in the way he cared for his father's sheep. He would protect them no matter what the cost. That was his responsibility. His thinking was, *The sheep belong to my father, so I can't lose one!*

David brought this same sense of responsibility to the battlefield. He did not emerge as God's man because he killed Goliath. David's actions to defeat Goliath were the natural result of his principles. It was his character that made him fearless. He was committed to doing the right thing regardless of personal cost.

But moral rectitude was not enough. Many people live upright lives yet do nothing for God. To explain David, we must delve deeper than that. David wanted to *know* God and not just know about God. As we read the psalms (half of them are written by David), we discover his thinking, his commentary on the world, how he gained perspective by praising the Almighty and how he released his emotions. Let's look at four examples:

> You, O LORD, are a shield about me, my glory, and the lifter of my head.
>
> Psalm 3:3

You have given me relief when I was in distress. Be gracious to me and hear my prayer!

Psalm 4:1

I will give thanks to the LORD with my whole heart; I will recount all of your wonderful deeds.

Psalm 9:1

The fool says in his heart, "There is no God." . . . The LORD looks down from heaven on the children of man, to see if there are any who understand, who seek after God.

Psalm 14:1–2

God looked for a man who would act solely as His representative with no other motive. Until he reached the battlefield and saw Goliath, David may not have realized that God needed a victory. But God let him know that he should act on His behalf.

This must be the reason for any initiative in spiritual battle. To carry out God's will, our motivation must have heaven's endorsement.

For Reflection

Why would you say you are a man or woman after God's heart? If you cannot say you are a person after God's heart, how can you change that?

5

What to Do with the Wrong Message

Behold, the champion, the Philistine of Gath, Goliath by name, came up out of the ranks of the Philistines and spoke the same words as before. And David heard him. All the men of Israel, when they saw the man, fled from him and were much afraid.

1 Samuel 17:23–24

Finally, we reach the battlefield. David is exactly where God wants him to be. But David does not understand yet what to do. How will he find out? How will he discern God's will?

David only knows he has the duty, which his father gave him, and he is determined to fulfill it. He arrives just as the

47

Israelite army is moving into battle formation. They are shouting war cries, lining up in their ranks, heading to the frontline. This was not a good time to deliver Jesse's presents to his brothers or their commander. David is logical, and he stores the goods with the one who manages supplies. He then joins the crowd. Who knows what he might see!

David does what any eager boy would do. He goes through the crowd and finds his brothers. "Dad sent me with food," he reports.

"Great," says Eliab. "We're sick of army rations. Now, get out of our way. We have a battle to fight."

Except, as we already know, there was no fight. Instead, guess who emerges—again. Here comes Goliath. For the first time, David hears what the others have heard eighty times.

The people of Israel faced two enemies. One external, the other internal. The external enemy was obvious. Has there ever been a more imposing soldier than Goliath? His defenses were impregnable, his weapons awesome. Plus, he was backed by an overpowering army.

The internal enemy was more devastating. The people cowered in fear. They were defeated before the fight. That is what fear does. Where was the confidence of Joshua's armies when the Israelites conquered the land? They had forgotten the promises of God. Fear had robbed them of the peaceful, victorious and prosperous life that God clearly intended for His people.

Why did David not flee in fear? David was courageous because he had a different perspective. The shepherd boy cannot control the giant's words. Neither can we avoid hearing the words of the enemy. He shouts his messages constantly through the media and internet. We can, however, filter those words through God's Word. We can be people of The Book. David did not see a hopeless situation because he knew this giant was no match for his God. Further, David knew this God personally, which gave him the confidence his countrymen lacked.

What would David do with the words he heard? He did not try to argue with Goliath. Words were useless against the giant. Besides, Goliath's words were backed up by serious power. Argue with him and he would squash you without a second thought.

Neither was David intimidated by the words of his brothers. Eliab spoke for them when he ridiculed David and told him to go back home and take care of that measly little flock of sheep. Intimidation is still a major tool the devil uses today. He shouts insults at Christians through the media. Intimidation becomes humiliation. Those closest to us inform us that we are worthless. We should not even try. Resistance is futile.

We Christians may try to ignore the messages that surround us, but that is virtually impossible. Some of us may respond with a harsh criticism or recite biblical platitudes that others do not believe and do not want to hear. Some demand that society adhere to a standard they no longer embrace. We may criticize those who are attempting to make a difference if their theology does not match ours. We assume God could not possibly use them because of that. Many Christians argue constantly about God and His ways. But their arguing makes me wonder, *Do they really know God?*

There were several reasons David knew this was his battle. He knew the words of Goliath were definitely not of God. He saw the effect of Goliath's words on Israel—cowering in fear was not how God's people should behave. The Spirit of God was residing in David. He knew God and therefore recognized when the Spirit was moving him to take action.

This was the moment for which God had prepared David. He knew it in his spirit.

For Reflection

What messages from the culture (from television, publications, music, social media) intimidate you? What lies is the enemy shouting at you? How can you resist those messages?

6

A Crazy Idea

David said to Saul, ". . . Your servant will go and fight with this Philistine."

1 Samuel 17:32

David stood before King Saul. "Don't you worry anymore," he said. "I'll fight the giant."

What a bold (stupid?) statement to make. Such confidence. Almost cocky! Does David even know what he is saying? I am not sure he does. He is acting under the compulsion of the Spirit. He is defending the honor of God. He knows something must be done, and if no one else steps forward, he concludes that God must have called him to do the job.

51

David has no weapons with which to fight the giant, but he is confident, though not in himself. His confidence is in God. He believes God has prepared him for this conflict; therefore, God will use him as he is—a shepherd. Still, he appears before King Saul and makes his case. He will go into battle with the backing of royal authority.

Too many people feel God cannot use them as they are. They are convinced they have to get a certain degree, they need to know influential people or they must have a decent-sized bank account. A certain title after their name (Ph.D., CEO, Chief-something) would not hurt. Only then do they believe that God will use them. But there is always someone with a more prestigious degree, a wider network, a bigger bank account or a fancier title.

Besides, the moment you are conscious of your abilities, it becomes unlikely that God will get the credit.

David was not awed with the trappings of royal power, nor was he swayed by the outward appearance of the enemy. The size of the man, big or small, made no difference. Perhaps a plan had already started to form in his mind. He may have been thinking, *The bigger the man, the bigger the target.*

Goliath can either scare you as he did all the Israelites, or you can think, *He's so big, I can't miss!* Maybe David was thinking about all the years he had practiced with the sling. He had chased off many a wild animal flinging stones with great accuracy. Big or small made no difference. Just one stone had to get through a hole in Goliath's helmet. That was the giant's weak spot. David revealed none of these thoughts.

Logic must have told Saul this was madness. Look at this scrawny kid. He has no armor. He has no weapons. He has no training. But Saul had no memory. He did not remember that a year or two before, a servant had told him about this shepherd who was "a man of war." He did not remember that David played soothing music for him, or that David was one of his armor-bearers—how many did he have anyway? He certainly was not paying attention to the fact that God's Spirit was in David.

David must, of course, make a case that he is indeed the person to fight Goliath. Saul rightly notes the downsides of the idea: You are just a kid, and Goliath is a trained warrior. David is a person of humility but here he needs to reveal that he has fought and defeated the lion and the bear. "This uncircumcised Philistine shall be like one of them" (verse 36).

Why? Not because David is Goliath's equal. Not because his earlier experience guaranteed success. No, David makes Saul understand the reason. "He has defied the armies of the living God." That is the reason David must fight him.

Then David hammered home the point. It is not about me. It is about God. "The LORD who delivered me from the paw of the lion and from the paw of the bear will deliver me from the hand of this Philistine" (verse 37). Faith radiates with a minimum of words. This is the powerful witness of the Spirit. David's testimony and proclamation gave him confidence and inspired King Saul. David elevated the battle to a spiritual level and made it God's cause.

This argument got through to Saul. At one point early in his reign, the king had known the power of God. He had lost that power, but he recognized it in the teenager. Thus, he thought, *Maybe, just maybe, this will work. It is crazy, but what other options do I have?*

"Go," ordered Saul, "and the LORD be with you!"

The one who has dismissed God in his own life is now totally depending on God to rescue him and his army through a teenage boy.

For Reflection

How do you take the focus off your own abilities and remain humble, trusting only in God's abilities?

1

Who Is Elijah?

Now Elijah the Tishbite, of Tishbe in Gilead, said to Ahab, "As the LORD, the God of Israel, lives, before whom I stand."

1 Kings 17:1

Elijah was a man with a nature like ours, and he prayed fervently that it might not rain, and for three years and six months it did not rain on the earth. Then he prayed again, and heaven gave rain, and the earth bore its fruit.

James 5:17–18

Elijah explodes on the scene without any introduction except the name of his hometown. There is no dramatic vision like

Isaiah who saw God sitting on His throne. There is no clarion call like Jeremiah who received a word as a teenager. We know nothing about his parents, unlike Samuel, who was the answer to his mother's prayer. Or John the Baptist, whose father received a personal message from the angel Gabriel in the Temple.

We do, however, know something very important: Elijah stands before Israel's God. That is the source of his authority. The fact that his audience, Israel's King Ahab, no longer acknowledges Elijah's God adds to the drama.

Here is another important fact: We know Elijah was a person just like us. That is what James says in his epistle. Elijah prayed fervently that it would not rain. Result: no rain for three and a half years. Then he prayed again, and what do you know: It rained!

If Elijah was an ordinary person like you and me, then I want to learn the secret of his prayer life. I want to know how he survived three-plus years of isolation, and how he found the courage to confront a powerful monarch and 450 prophets of Baal on Mount Carmel. Perhaps he can teach us how we can be God's powerful tools in our hostile surroundings.

But we are rushing ahead too quickly. Let's start where the writer of 1 Kings starts. Elijah was a Tishbite from Gilead, a land belonging to the half tribe of Manasseh east of the Jordan River. We are told he wore a garment of hair with a belt of leather (see 2 Kings 1:8). He must have looked rather wild. He probably did not own a razor. He is usually depicted visually as having an unruly beard. The first recorded words out of this wild character's mouth were to King Ahab. "There will be no rain or dew for three years . . . unless I say so" (see 1 Kings 17:1).

How could Elijah make such a bold, radical, provocative statement? The prophet broadcasts his authority: "As the LORD, the God of Israel lives." You do not make such a declaration unless you know this God. Not intellectually. I mean really *know* God personally and experience Him deeply so that you recognize His voice when He speaks to you.

The more you know God, the more you can understand the culture in which you live. For Elijah the problem is clear. Baal is an imposter. The Israelites trusted the supposed god of nature who caused rain that watered the crops and produced abundant harvests. Elijah pronounces that there will be no harvest because there will be no rain.

This was a declaration of war against Baal!

Clearly Elijah does not tolerate the popular culture. Speaking for Israel's authentic God, Elijah challenges Ahab and the population of Israel to see just how well Baal, the pretender, provides for their needs.

One more important detail about Elijah is his name. It means "My God is the Lord." Elijah more than lives up to that identity. The prophet does not simply make a faith declaration. He lives out his name in a hostile culture. He is definitely not politically correct. He refuses to tolerate the prevalent thinking of the day. He will not surrender authority to a blatantly pagan and immoral ruler and his ruthless wife.

This is the ultimate spiritual contest.

For Reflection

Elijah was an ordinary person like you. His identity was "My God is the Lord." If God is your Lord, what do these two facts tell you about your place in the world today?

2

Ready to Pay the Price

As the LORD, the God of Israel, lives, before whom I stand, there shall be neither dew nor rain these years, except by my word.

1 Kings 17:1

I believe some, perhaps many, in Israel were uncomfortable with Baal worship. But what could they do? Not much, they thought. It did not make sense to rock the boat. Do not buck the system; just get on with life. In other words, the population at large surrendered to a lie. As a result, they were going to suffer. They were going to go hungry from famine and be thirsty because of lack of water. Would they wake up and do something? Unfortunately, no! Their true identity was supposedly in almighty God, but their behavior denied that reality.

The prevailing culture challenges us as well today. We hear many say, "Jesus is Lord," but is He really Lord? Is He really in charge of your life, of my life? How do we know?

As Christians, we are challenged to radical living. Elijah defines *radical* as simply meaning that God totally rules his life. Whatever God commands, Elijah obeys. This forces Elijah to stand up to a hostile system that he cannot possibly change unless God enters the picture and takes action.

Who is standing up to our culture today? Who will challenge the many lies we are hearing?

There is a desire among many Christians for approval by the world. Elijah did not seek such an endorsement. He provoked. He antagonized. He made enemies. In the process, he revealed the power and glory of God; however, he paid a price for this stand. The cost was suffering—something we prefer to avoid. Because Elijah took a stand, he endured hunger, loneliness, isolation and even depression. He had to flee his people and be hunted by King Ahab, ultimately questioning his mission.

Today, the Church of Jesus Christ must be ready to suffer for the mission God has given her. In the free West, we do not like that, but in many countries, the Church is hated and persecuted. In fact, one in six people who identify as Christians experience high levels of persecution for their faith.[1]

In the two most populated countries on earth, Christians live in a surveillance state. In China, an estimated 97 million Christians can be tracked through facial recognition software and more than 415 million surveillance cameras. Attendance at church will be monitored. India plans to introduce similar facial recognition surveillance, which will make it easier for Hindu extremists to attack converts to Christianity.[2]

Meanwhile violent attacks against our brothers and sisters continue to increase. In 2019, nearly 10,000 churches or Christian buildings were attacked, and an average of eight Christians each day were killed for their faith. Another 3,711 Christians were arrested and imprisoned without trial. In Iraq and Syria, Christianity is on the verge of disappearing.[3]

You may respond that such persecution is not happening where you live. Will that always be true? Israel lived in the Promised Land where rain fell at the right time every year to produce abundant harvests. Elijah reminded them that God provided the rain. And God could shut it off.

Maybe we take God's blessings for granted. Do we consider that He could shut off those blessings as well?

Paul explains persecution, saying that we are being asked to participate and fill up that which is lacking in the sufferings of Christ (see Colossians 1:24). Elijah will demonstrate how that works.

For Reflection

As you look at the world around you, where does conflict touch your life? What would you like for God to show you as you study the example of Elijah?

3

Speaking God's Word

The word of the LORD came to him. . . . So he went and did according to the word of the LORD.

1 Kings 17:2, 5

Elijah's initial moment in the spotlight did not last long. Immediately after his bold proclamation to King Ahab, Elijah went into hiding and disappeared from public ministry for three years.

Still, the Word of the Lord came to Elijah. Do we have any idea how great a privilege it is for those to whom the Word of God comes? Who am I that the Word of God would come to me? Elijah was special. Or was he?

You and I are here today equipped with God's Word! It has been my privilege to deliver Bibles to people who are deprived of the Word of God because of government restrictions. Do you realize that there are more unevangelized people in the world today, people unreached with the Gospel, than ever before? Many of them are illiterate. But they can hear, and we have the Word. We have the liberty of going with the Word to any dark area in the world. With one caveat: We need to realize that we may not come back!

Perhaps that is the issue; we want some assurance of safety. Where is that found in Scripture? Certainly not in the example of Elijah. Safety was not his concern.

Elijah declared "As the Lord, the God of Israel lives, there will be no rain." That is the power of proclamation. Hearing from the Lord is where Elijah starts. And that is where we must start. Smart academics may declare otherwise—that God does not exist and therefore He has nothing to say. Actually, I think they are fools. Scripture agrees. "The fool says in his heart, 'There is no God'" (Psalm 14:1). I do not care what "evidence" they present or indoctrination by which they may try to brainwash me. God is alive! He is the one before whom I stand.

That is not safe, but it sure is exciting.

There are too many Christians who live as practical atheists. Nothing distinguishes them from the world. When we fit nicely into the world, the devil leaves us alone.

Elijah was radical. We might even say that he was reckless. He operated contrary to the prevailing culture of his day. He most certainly was not conformed to this world. There were others who believed God existed, but they kept their opinions private. Better not to upset the current power brokers. Who could possibly debate King Ahab (not to mention his strong-willed wife, Jezebel) and the numerous prophets of Baal? Their sheer numbers would overwhelm any single voice. Why stick your neck out—and get your head chopped off?

This courageous prophet had a different perspective. Because he knew God, he was not afraid to deliver God's message.

Have you ever consciously stood before God and waited for Him until you heard Him speak to your heart? Have you received His anointing, His Spirit, His compassion or His courage? They are all available to us, because God is alive, and we can stand before Him.

We call the Bible God's Word. When we read Scripture and receive it as God's Word to us, it becomes our Word. As we absorb God's Word, words from our mouths become God's words. The two intertwine. Indeed, God desires to speak through us.

In Old Testament times, God spoke through a few prophets, like Elijah. Now God speaks through His Son. And His Son, Jesus, is in you (I hope!); therefore, God can speak through you—if you let Him.

The life of Jesus, wherever you take that life, is where God is going to speak. You can carry the life of Jesus into a situation where Jesus is officially banned. My friends who live under severe persecution do it all the time. They are Jesus among religious fanatics and hostile governments.

Wherever Jesus wants to go, He can send you. Do you agree? Wherever you go, there Jesus goes. No one can stop Jesus! You do not need any special equipment. You do not even need—please do not misunderstand me here—a physical Bible. If the living and written Word fills you, then your word is the Word of God.

The secret to the courage Elijah displayed is that he stood before the God who lives. That should be our secret, too.

For Reflection

Today or tomorrow, as you read the Bible, picture yourself standing before Jesus listening for His Word to you. What is He saying? Where can you go with this message? Who needs to experience the presence of Jesus in you now?

Training for Battle

So he went and did according to the word of the LORD. He went and lived by the brook Cherith that is east of the Jordan. . . .

Then the word of the LORD came to him, "Arise, go to Zarephath, which belongs to Sidon, and dwell there. Behold, I have commanded a widow there to feed you."

1 Kings 17:5, 8–9

We must recognize that Elijah could do nothing about the problems of Israel. The key to understanding this story—and

67

this is true of every Old Testament hero—is to realize that Elijah did what he couldn't.

No one can do what Elijah did, unless . . .

- she or he is called by God
- she or he has the discipline to listen for God to speak and then follow His instructions
- she or he is willing to train, preparing for however long it takes for the moment when God opens up the door for a wider influence

We prefer to rush to Mount Carmel. We are awed by the faith of Elijah and the great victory over the prophets of Baal. We are eager to go and demonstrate our faith. That is not how God works with His ministers, those who are truly effective in His work. A season of preparation is necessary, often lasting years and involving time in what I call the wilderness. God may require a lifetime of preparation for you to give one minute of supreme service for Him in which you challenge evil and emerge victorious.

We must be patient. There are periods of solitude and suffering as God's chosen servant learns to recognize and obey His voice. This time is never wasted—it is vital to God's plans to use us.

Elijah's training regimen began during a famine. His first public appearance before King Ahab created an ecological disaster and disrupted the economy of Israel. There would be no rain. At first the population probably had enough resources from their most recent harvest. Then the spring rains did not come and the seeds they planted produced just a few pitiful shoots. There was no rain in the fall, and no harvest. On and on the drought dragged until the situation was dire.

Famine is a devastating experience. Often it is man-made. As we write this, children are dying of hunger in Yemen, victims of a brutal civil war waged by the Houthi rebels against the Saudi-backed Yemeni government. The combatants do not have enough compassion to cease their conflict for the good of the people they claim to govern.

When I was a boy, six million Ukrainians died from man-made famine because Stalin wanted to impose Communism on them. He used this to break their resistance. During World War II, my country, the Netherlands, suffered terribly in the winter of 1944 during German occupation. A German blockade cut off fuel and food shipments from farms to the cities. An estimated 22,000 died, mostly elderly citizens.[1] Fortunately, I did not starve because I lived in a farming village.

Elijah was not exempt from the consequences of God's judgment on Israel. But God also provided for him, sending him across the Jordan to a secluded spot with water. God provided food, delivered by RAS—that is Raven Air Service—twice each day. Eventually the water source dried up and God moved Elijah to Sidon, north of Israel, to the home of a desperate widow who was preparing to cook the last meal for herself and her son before they died of starvation. God miraculously provided for the three of them.

Why this drama? God could have provided Elijah with water from a rock and manna, the bread of angels, every morning. He had done that before. But God does not work by formulas. He puts us in situations where we must depend on Him, waiting for Him to supply a unique solution. In this case, the prophet needed to see God miraculously provide in a single home so he would learn that God would also work miracles in the national setting.

If Elijah was going to be effective challenging the prevailing system, he had to go through God's training program.

For Reflection

How badly do you want to be used by God? What price are you willing to pay? Do you recognize His training regimen? Take note of what He is doing, thank Him and express your willingness to be His tool for service in His Kingdom.

5

A "Little" Miracle

She said to Elijah, "What have you against me, O man of
God?" . . . The woman said to Elijah, "Now I know that you
are a man of God, and that the word of the LORD in your
mouth is truth."

1 Kings 17:18, 24

Part One of Elijah's training occurred in solitude. Part Two
was more challenging. When his water source dried up, Elijah
was sent by God to Zarephath, a city on the Mediterranean
Coast in the region of Sidon.

I think Elijah liked the quiet isolation of Cherith brook.
Life was simple. God delivered groceries daily and the creek

provided water anytime day or night. But God never leaves us in solitude. We need others. When the water supply shut down, God moved the prophet about one hundred miles northwest where a widow would meet his needs. Not a Jewish woman—she was a Gentile. This fact angered people centuries later when Jesus mentioned it at His home synagogue in Nazareth.

Zarephath was located in Sidon, the birthplace of Queen Jezebel. God placed Elijah in the heart of Baal country and demonstrated that He is greater than the local deity. This was a warm-up for the main event on Mount Carmel.

Elijah was placed in a family in dire need. We do not know how the woman's husband died, but she had a son to care for and apparently no extended family able to help her. When Elijah entered the city and met her for the first time, he asked for a glass of water, which she graciously gave. Then he asked her for a piece of bread. That is when she revealed her predicament.

To our ears, Elijah's next request sounds selfish and unreasonable. "First make me a little cake . . . and afterward make something for yourself and your son" (1 Kings 17:13). How could he? She had just told him that she barely had enough for herself and her son. Could he not let them eat together and then die with some dignity?

But Elijah was acting on God's orders. Besides meeting his material needs, Elijah was bearing witness to an unreached woman. Elijah was sent to assist her transformation from an outsider to one who recognizes the only true God. This is a spiritual skirmish. Soon the drama will move south and explode in a titanic spiritual battle on a national scale.

Our aim in any missionary endeavor is to follow Jesus as we are armed with passion for the Word and compassion for the world. Elijah was not called to reach the nation of Sidon. He learned compassion by caring for one distraught Sidonese widow. This was God's work. When Elijah made the initial request of the widow, he promised that if she complied, from that point forward she would not run out of flour or oil for the duration of the drought. Only God could do that.

Sometime later, the boy became ill and died. Surely during those weeks or months Elijah became attached to the child. His hostess, of course, was distraught. "What have you against me, O man of God?" (verse 18).

What could Elijah do? When in history had a dead person ever been raised back to life? Out of compassion and in desperation, Elijah called out, "O LORD my God, have you brought calamity even upon the widow with whom I sojourn, by killing her son?" (verse 20).

Do not criticize Elijah for blaming God. Elijah figured that if God claimed the child, He could also return him to life. He was thinking like the patriarch Abraham who "considered that God was able even to raise [his son, Isaac] from the dead" (Hebrews 11:19). Then Elijah stretched himself out over the child and prayed, "Let this child's life come into him again" (verse 21).

God answered Elijah's prayer. The child was restored to life. When Elijah carried the boy down to his mother, she joyfully said, "Now I know that you are a man of God, and that the word of the LORD in your mouth is truth" (verse 24). She was now a believer.

We readily are drawn to the spectacular. But for this woman, the miracle with her son was more significant than God burning up a water-drenched sacrifice on Mount Carmel.

Our response in crisis, large or small, will only be the outcome of our daily walk with God. I have often said that I never wanted to lead a large organization that spans the globe. If I had known what God had planned, I would never have made my first trip to Poland in 1955. But God knows we cannot handle a big vision initially. He led Elijah one step at a time. He did the same with me.

Allow God to lead you and prepare you for whatever unique assignment He has planned for you. And do it in His timing.

For Reflection

Is there one person or a family to whom God would like for you to go and demonstrate His power and provision? If so, pray for them and ask for Him to lead you.

6

It's Time

After many days the word of the LORD came to Elijah, in the third year, saying, "Go, show yourself to Ahab, and I will send rain upon the earth."

1 Kings 18:1

Finally, something is about to happen. Rain is coming. The famine will end.

Not so fast! Too often we make plans for God, thinking that it is better to do something than to sit around.

Did Elijah get impatient? I do not think so. He waited for God to direct him.

Al has a mug with this thought: "The one who hurries delays the things of God." I do not want to suggest that planning is wrong; however, our plans should always be crafted in a context of prayer, patience and discernment. Sadly, our tendency is to throw up a quick prayer and then rush into action or rush to formulate a strategy and then ask God to bless it.

We cannot say how much Elijah knew when he emerged from hiding. He understood he had to confront King Ahab, who by now was desperate for a solution to the severe drought. I doubt the prophet knew more than that—God by His Spirit probably revealed what Elijah needed to do one step at a time. So Elijah goes to meet the king and runs across Obadiah, a believer in Elijah's God. Obadiah was what we would call a secret believer. He hid one hundred of God's prophets to save them from the murderous wrath of Queen Jezebel.

Ahab's right-hand man reveals that his master has searched all of the surrounding nations for Elijah. That had to include Sidon just to the north of Israel. It makes sense that Ahab would consult with his father-in-law. Logic also suggests that Elijah would never hide in the heart of Baal worship. How clever. Our Lord is so creative!

There is no escaping the danger of pursuing Christ's commission. A life of faith is required every step of the way. God will sustain you and hide you or save you, whatever is necessary, until you fulfill your God-given mission. That is why Elijah was not captured despite Ahab's thorough search. That did not, however, guarantee Elijah's future safety.

Obadiah calls his boss. King Ahab comes and immediately accuses Elijah, calling him the troubler of Israel. Actually, Ahab has it backward. Elijah answers, "I have not troubled Israel, but you have, and your father's house, because you have abandoned the commandments of the LORD and followed the Baals" (1 Kings 18:18). Ahab cannot argue with the prophet. He has just been confronted with the facts.

I wonder if this is when God revealed the next step. It was time for a confrontation to establish who was really the divine ruler of Israel. Elijah commanded Ahab to send messengers and gather all the prophets of Baal and Asherah "who eat at Jezebel's table." Now that takes guts.

Perhaps you are not comfortable at this point. We generally prefer to avoid confrontation. We want peace and comfort. That desire is good, but not if that means peace on our terms. Elijah wanted peace on God's terms.

Most likely we are also uncomfortable with any actions that go against the laws of the land. Peter tells us in his first epistle to submit "to every human institution, whether it be to the emperor . . . or to governors." (1 Peter 2:13–14). Yet Peter defied the Jewish rulers, declaring, "We must obey God rather than men" (Acts 5:29). Specifically, Peter obeyed the command of Jesus to go into all the world and make disciples even when that opposed government authorities.

Amazingly, Ahab sent out invitations for a command appearance at Mount Carmel. Perhaps he was overconfident. The devil was so sure he would win, he accepted the invitation.

We Christians proclaim that there is another Kingdom. This automatically means there will be opposition. Persecution has one objective—to silence the voice of God, which is why there must eventually be a confrontation.

Why does the Chinese government continue to tear down crosses, arrest pastors and close churches? These congregations are not challenging the government's authority. But the Chinese Communist Party rightly intuits that the real agenda of the Church is to introduce and build the Kingdom of God. They cannot allow any competition to Communist rule. Even though Christians pray for their leaders and obey the laws, the Church is perceived as a threat.

It is the same in many other places. Even in the West.

Elijah was not willing to play by King Ahab's politics and rules. He was about to confront the power center of Israel. In the process, he would challenge the hearts of the people.

For Reflection

Where does the Church in your nation threaten the authority of the government? Is there any situation in which you might need to disobey the law of your country in order to obey a clear command of God?

1

God Speaks—
Are We Listening?

The word of the LORD came to Jonah the son of Amittai.

Jonah 1:1

How did Jonah receive this word?

It might have started on a cool evening sometime between 780 and 750 BC while Jonah relaxed on his back patio. Life was good for this prophet. Other prophets railed against the people and proclaimed God's judgment. They were persecuted and even killed because their messages were so unpopular (see Luke 11:47–52.) But Jonah was popular with the people and the political establishment. His message to King Jeroboam II was that God would restore the lost borders of Israel (see 2 Kings 14:25). Finally, some good news after so many defeats! Then he saw his prophecy fulfilled. He was welcome anytime in the king's court. He had real political influence.

"Jonah!" the voice called. *Probably one of my neighbors or a cousin*, he thought. *Could they not leave me alone at the end of a long, hot day?* But the rules of hospitality required that you never leave your neighbor standing outside, not even in the middle of the night. Who knows? Maybe he had some unexpected guests who needed bread.

"Come in," Jonah answered.

"Jonah!"

Oh no! That was neither his neighbor, nor his cousin. This was . . . his Boss! He had better get out of his chair and answer.

"Yes, Lord."

He knew when the Lord started speaking; he was a prophet after all. There were not many prophets in Jonah's time. Actually, it seemed as if God did not speak much anymore, and it surely showed in the life of the nation. Despite recent military gains, there were enemies inside and outside Israel's borders. Whether you looked at things from an economic, moral or spiritual perspective, there was little cause for rejoicing.

The name *Jonah* means "dove," which is the symbol of the Holy Spirit who searches the very depths of our hearts. Jonah's job as a prophet was to submit to the Holy Spirit. Instead, as we will soon see, Jonah argued with God.

How do we respond when we hear the Word of the Lord? A Russian pastor, during the years when Bibles were not allowed to be printed in the Soviet Union, in answer to prayer received a copy of the Bible. Eagerly he ripped out pages and distributed portions of Scripture to each person in his church. The next day the pastor was in town and saw a member of his congregation with a big smile. "You must have gotten a good page," said the pastor.

"Oh yes," said the man. "I received a page from Jeremiah!"

"That gloomy prophet," said the pastor. "He preached his heart out and never saw any results. I have a page from Matthew. Why don't we swap?"

The man said, "Oh no, pastor. Listen to what this says. 'The Word of the Lord came to Jeremiah.' If the Word of the Lord can come to Jeremiah, it can come to me, too!"

God spoke to Jonah because Jonah had a relationship with God. God also speaks to us if we have a relationship with Him. Are we listening? Do we hear Him? Are we eager to receive God's Word? Are we ready to obey it?

Or are our heads filled with noise? Are the headphones of an MP3 player or smartphone constantly plugged into our ears? Must we always have the television on in the room? Are our schedules filled to overflowing with meetings and activities? If so, how will we know when God is speaking to us?

What are the consequences if we miss God's Word to us? They could be catastrophic—eternity may hang in the balance for millions of souls.

For Reflection

Can you hear God's voice in your life? Or is there too much outside noise? How can you reduce the noise in order to hear God more clearly? How do you recognize God's voice?

2

The Compassion Gap

"Go to the great city of Nineveh and preach against it, because its wickedness has come up before me." But Jonah ran away from the LORD and headed for Tarshish. He went down to Joppa, where he found a ship bound for that port. After paying the fare, he went aboard and sailed for Tarshish to flee from the LORD.

Jonah 1:2–3 NIV

Try to understand Jonah's problem. He was ordered to go to the enemy of his people. The Assyrians were making forays into northern Israel where Jonah lived. It is entirely possible that they had attacked his home village of Gath-hepher.

Perhaps Assyrians had killed his mother and father. Maybe he had watched soldiers rape his sisters. If that is the case, we can certainly understand why Jonah hated this assignment. Being told to go to Nineveh would be like being ordered today to go to Baghdad. Or Mogadishu. Or Pyongyang, North Korea.

Maybe your enemies are closer to home. Perhaps it is the abortion provider in your community. Or the drug dealer who has ensnared too many students in your high school. It could be the neighbor who loudly promotes the political candidate who opposes everything you consider Christian.

Jonah should have been pleased to learn that the wickedness of Nineveh had come to God's attention. Jonah believed the Assyrians should have been judged for their brutality. His solution: Go—and kill them!

God has a different message. Go—and *win* them.

We do not live in a friendly environment. I certainly do not in Holland. There is a lot of bad news in the papers each day. There is plenty of anti-Christian sentiment throughout the country. Though I live in a town with many churches, there are also several mosques. On Friday afternoons in my office, I often hear the call to prayer from the minaret.

When I go shopping at the Saturday market, there are numerous Muslim families in the crowd—you can easily recognize them by the way the men walk and because the women wear headscarves.

What do they think of Christians? Are they being greeted by us with a smile and a hearty "Good morning"?

It is easier to identify with Jonah than with any other prophet. Others feel so holy. Jonah is so much like us.

God says: Go ye!

Jonah says: No!

Jonah's basic problem: He had too much love for *himself*. He thought: *God will make a fool of me. I will lose face.* He refused to be a fool for Christ. He wanted God, but not God's Kingdom. He wanted blessing without responsibility. He had no compassion for the lost. He was more than willing to let them go to hell.

What Jonah did have was money. He had made some wise investments. Rather than going east to Iraq, he headed west and bought a ticket on a Mediterranean cruise. He figured it was his money and he could spend it any way he chose. He did not stop to think that all we have in our bank accounts and investment portfolio belongs to God. Jonah pays with God's money to escape from God's call.

There is a burden on us. It is called the Great Commission. "Go therefore and make disciples of all nations" (Matthew 28:19). I believe God has called enough people in each generation to fulfill the Great Commission in their lifetime. But too many have run away.

Where is our compassion? God is not willing that *any* should perish! That applies to Nineveh and Amsterdam and New York. We are responsible for the Ninevehs of this world.

Jonah ran because he saw opportunities as an enemy instead of seeing the enemy as his biggest opportunity. What opportunities do you see today to reach out to people you might consider enemies?

You have to be divine to make friends with your enemies.

For Reflection

Do you have compassion for the lost? If so, what is the evidence and what are you doing about it? If you do not have compassion for the lost, why not? What opportunities do you see today to reach out to people who might be considered your enemies?

3

Why God Sent a Storm

But the LORD hurled a great wind upon the sea, and there was a mighty tempest on the sea, so that the ship threatened to break up.

Jonah 1:4

Jonah boarded the ship and heaved a sigh of relief. He had done it! He had run away from God, and God had not stopped him. No way was he going to those dreaded Assyrians in Nineveh. If God wanted to send those terrorists a message, He could find someone else to deliver it.

Jonah stood on the bow and watched as the city of Joppa faded into the distance. He loved the feeling of wind on his face. It was a beautiful evening, and the clouds were full of rich red and orange color as the sun set into the Mediterranean Sea. He could smell dinner being prepared in the galley. He would be eating at the captain's table. This was the life. Then he turned his attention to the black clouds forming to the north.

"Looks like we are headed into a storm," said one of the sailors behind him.

A pang of fear stabbed him. Was this the moment when Jonah began to suspect that he was in trouble? We can run from God, but we cannot hide. One of the messages clearly communicated throughout the book of Jonah is God's sovereignty over nature.

"The LORD hurled a great wind" (1:4).

"The LORD appointed a great fish to swallow up Jonah" (1:17).

"The LORD spoke to the fish, and it vomited Jonah out upon the dry land" (2:10).

"The LORD God appointed a plant and made it come up over Jonah" (4:6).

"God appointed a worm that attacked the plant, so that it withered" (4:7).

"God appointed a scorching east wind" (4:8).

God has total control over nature. God's creation knows God's voice and obeys His commands. He spoke to the fish because the fish would not argue with Him. Creation is God's tool to get Jonah back on the right track. God did not send a storm to pester Jonah. God sent the storm to save Nineveh.

Jonah was in the wrong location: He should have been walking on solid ground toward Nineveh rather than staggering on the roiling sea.

Jonah was with the wrong company: He should have been meeting with Nineveh's sinners and seekers instead of a crew of cursing sailors. Sure the sailors were religious—in times of crisis we all are! They also needed a message from God. Unfortunately, God's messenger was not available. While the mariners cried out to their gods and tried to save the ship, Jonah slept. The sailors were amazed that a man with such a bad conscience could sleep so well!

Jonah had a wrong theology: God cares for Jews only.

He had a wrong attitude toward Gentiles: Get lost! (Doing nothing or running away is the same as saying "Get lost.")

But God loves lost people, so He gives Jonah a second chance.

It is the same today—you also have another chance. God has not written off the world. Or you. Or the person you are going to meet in your "Nineveh."

Question: Has the world passed the point of no return?

I do not believe that it has. There is still hope. God can change a city, a society and a nation. What will it take for us to wake up and realize that *now* is the time for us to announce God's solution to a desperate world? Maybe more natural disasters—earthquakes, hurricanes, tornadoes, wildfires or tsunamis? Another pandemic? Must we first endure another riot or a more horrific terrorist attack? Is that what is necessary to wake us up?

Answer: "Who knows?" (Jonah 3:9). God knows, and He is calling *you*. You may not know the answers. But you can know God—His character, His love. That is enough, provided that you recognize His voice. "It's horrible . . . to die in captivity, but it's worse to be free and to sleep, and sleep, and sleep."[1]

For Reflection

Are you living life as if the world has passed the point of no return? Or are you looking for opportunities in which you can contribute to the solution? What is one opportunity where you can make a difference now? Have you prayed and asked God what He would have you do?

4

Someone Has to Die

The sea was getting rougher and rougher. So they asked him, "What should we do to you to make the sea calm down for us?" "Pick me up and throw me into the sea," he replied, "and it will become calm. I know that it is my fault that this great storm has come upon you."

Jonah 1:11–12 NIV

Then they took Jonah and threw him overboard, and the raging sea grew calm. At this the men greatly feared the LORD, and they offered a sacrifice to the LORD and made vows to him.

Jonah 1:15–16 NIV

God says, "I am the Lord," meaning that He can send a storm on the sea or in your life. And God can still the storm—on the sea and in your life.

In order for the sailors to live, Jonah had to die. That much is clear. Unless Jonah fell into the sea and died, there would be no salvation for the sailors. Or for Nineveh.

Jesus said that in order to save your life, you have to lose it. So why did Jonah not just jump into the sea? Maybe he was not really willing to give up his life. Actually, Jonah is not going to commit suicide—that is never our call. The Christian life is radically different from the call of radical Islam. We are never asked to blow ourselves up and take as many people as possible with us. Jonah knows he has to die, but he cannot take his own life. Rather, he must offer up his life to save those of the sailors.

This is what I call sacramental living. We, too, must offer up our lives. We do that by giving up our rights so that others, who do not know Jesus, may have the right to hear the Good News of the Gospel.

Some may question the term "sacramental." I mean it in the sense that Paul explains in his letter to the Colossians: "In my flesh I am filling up what is lacking in Christ's afflictions for the sake of his body, that is, the church" (Colossians 1:24).

Jonah's words to the sailors: "Throw me into the sea." He was still a prophet. When he said the sea would become calm, he was speaking the truth.

Was Jonah's death the end or the beginning?

It was a beginning for the sailors. The sailors first prayed to their gods because Jonah did not give them reason to pray to his God. Then they rowed. That did not work, so they prayed to Jonah's God, and a miracle occurred. As a result, they sacrificed to the Lord God and made vows to Him. What kind of vows? Probably like the ones we make: Lord, if you save me from this mess, I will serve You for the rest of my life.

Unfortunately, we usually forget our vows when the problem is solved. Do not worry: God will remind you.

This was also the beginning of a new life for Jonah. Jesus said: "Unless a grain of wheat falls into the earth and dies, it remains alone; but if it dies, it bears much fruit" (John 12:24).

We all must die.

We must die to religion.

We must die to pride.

We must die to politics.

We must die to culture.

Only then can we begin again with real life in Christ.

Jonah is a type of Jesus—by voluntarily giving himself. Jonah is also an anti-type of Jesus—Jesus was innocent and crucified for the guilty. Jonah was guilty and was thrown overboard to save the "innocent."

This is sacramental living.

We always carry around in our body the death of Jesus, so that the life of Jesus may also be revealed in our body. For we who are alive are always being given over to death for Jesus' sake, so that his life may also be revealed in our mortal body. So then, death is at work in us, but life is at work in you.

2 Corinthians 4:10–12 NIV

This includes the willingness to come with a "self-destroying prophecy." Nineveh is lost. This city can only be saved if Jonah becomes a sacrament.

For Reflection

What would you do if in your community there was no church, no Bible, no Christian neighbors? This is not a theoretical question. There are places in the world today where Christians are isolated without any of the resources (buildings, literature or seminaries) that we take for granted. How could you reveal the life of Jesus in such a hostile society?

5

Time to Pray

From inside the fish Jonah prayed to the LORD his God. He said: "In my distress I called to the LORD, and he answered me. From deep in the realm of the dead I called for help, and you listened to my cry."

Jonah 2:1–2 NIV

The only answer God has for Nineveh's problem drowns.

This sacramental act of Jonah was not voluntary. But he was not a martyr. A martyr is a witness who has a choice—deny Christ and live, or proclaim Christ and be killed. There are many Christians killed each year because of their ethnicity or religion. There are a few martyrs who die with a witness for Jesus on their lips.

It has been my privilege to serve the Persecuted Church for more than sixty years. I have visited churches in the former Soviet Union, in China, in Cuba, in Colombia and in many Muslim countries. I have discovered that there is only one way to end persecution of Christians—stop talking about Jesus.

A few years ago, Al and I sat in the office of Shahbaz Bhatti in Islamabad. He was minister for minority affairs in Pakistan and the only Christian in President Musharef's cabinet. During lunch together, our friend told us that he had intentionally chosen to not marry. He did not want his wife and children to lose their father if or when he had to take a stand that might cost him his life.

I think he had a premonition. A year later, Bhatti publicly defended the legal rights of Asia Bibi, a Christian who was in prison, condemned to death after being accused of blasphemy. A few days later, he was ambushed and killed. He had prerecorded a message that was to be released in case of his death. In it he said, "I believe in Jesus Christ who has given His own life for us. . . . I am ready to die for a cause. I'm living for my community and suffering people, and I will die to defend their rights."[1]

If we want to see people reached for Jesus, to see the Gospel transform lives, there is a price that must be paid. The price is that we must give up our rights. We must live sacramentally. We must die to ourselves so that Christ can live through us.

I will never forget the last words spoken to me by Haik Hovsepian, an Iranian Armenian Protestant minister, after we spoke at a pastors' conference in Pakistan.

"Andrew, when they kill me, it will not be for being silent." Not if, but when. Two weeks later, he became a martyr.

Initiative that is translated into bold proclamation removes fear. When you hear God and follow His command, you can be sure that God will put you on the right path.

Do not believe what the devil tells you. The devil says that you will always be sinful, poor, sick, etc. While Jonah was in the belly of the fish, the devil said, "You will never get out of here. You will die in this smelly, stinking fish." The devil is a liar. Even when he speaks the truth. Never believe what the devil says.

———

How did Jonah feel in the fish? Desperate, no doubt.

Within the fish, Jonah could do only one thing: pray. So Jonah's greatest weakness became his greatest strength. He had lost everything. He could no longer run from God. In his distress, Jonah prayed. That was not strong enough. From the depths of the grave he prayed. Jonah cried for help, and God listened.

Jonah proves you can pray anytime, anywhere. God hears! And God does not laugh at Jonah's prayer.

He was running from the presence of God. But Jonah discovers that you cannot escape God's presence. "Where shall

I go from your Spirit?" wrote the psalmist. "Or where shall I flee from your presence? If I ascend to heaven, you are there! If I make my bed in Sheol, you are there" (Psalm 139:7–8). You cannot get more in the depths than Jonah, tossed wildly about as the fish swam through the turbulent sea.

It does not pay to run from God. I hope you are not running from God. Jesus will not stop you from running away, but it will be very lonely. It will be very dark. It will be very dangerous. Ultimately, you will not escape from Him.

For Reflection

Is God calling you? What is your answer? Are you running away from God? Why?

A Second Chance!

> Salvation belongs to the Lord!
>
> Jonah 2:9

> And the Lord spoke to the fish, and it vomited Jonah out upon the dry land.
>
> Jonah 2:10

> Then the word of the Lord came to Jonah the second time.
>
> Jonah 3:1

This is what we proclaim: Salvation comes from the Lord!

Genuine proclamation offers the solution to a problem. We have the answer to the problem of sin.

The wickedness of Nineveh came before the Lord. Today the sins of the world still come before God. Not generalities. Specific sins like stealing, murder, adultery, pride and not taking care of the poor. We all have sinned. I have sinned. I am not going to tell you my sins. Only that salvation is for my *specific* sins. For yours as well.

Why is the world rising up in protest against injustice? We demand answers to the problem of terrorism. To the problem of violence in schools. To racial inequities. More objections should be shouted against the problem of economic exploitation of brick workers in Pakistan. Against the sexual exploitation of women and children in many parts of the world.

We will not solve problems of violence with violence. We will not solve the problem of terrorism by simply killing terrorists. "The effect of righteousness will be peace, and the result of righteousness, quietness and trust forever" (Isaiah 32:17). For righteousness to take effect, there must first be repentance and a massive turning to God. That is why Jonah preached. That is why we must preach.

God sent Jonah to Nineveh to demonstrate what He wants to do with the whole world. First, there is judgment for our sins. Nineveh will be destroyed. Unless . . .

There is also forgiveness, if we repent. The demands of justice are fulfilled on the cross. This is our message!

But you ask how are you and how am I qualified to preach?

Look at the apostle Paul. He was least of the apostles (see 1 Corinthians 15:9). He was least of all the saints (see Ephesians

3:8). He was greatest of all sinners (see 1 Timothy 1:15). But he met the perfect Savior. That conferred his qualification.

Is that not our story? Are we not all called to give witness? Preaching is the function of the Church, which exists for the salvation of its nonmembers.

Maybe you have failed in this mission. Have you ever prayed for a second chance? You have come to a place of hopelessness because you did not pray, and now you wonder, *Will God give me another chance if I pray*?

Jonah prayed, and he received a second chance!

At the end of Jonah's prayer, the fish could no longer stomach Jonah. He vomited him onto the beach. How the prophet hugged the sand—he never thought he would feel solid ground beneath him again. He barely opened his eyes, then shut them again—the sun was so bright that his eyes had to adjust. Slowly he caught his breath. He turned over onto his back and squinted. What a beautiful sight—the Mediterranean Sea spread out before him. Not a cloud in the sky. No hint of a storm. He turned around and looked up at the trees lining the hills. That was even more beautiful—in fact, he would not mind if he never again set foot on a boat.

To one side was a stream, and Jonah went over to wash off the sand and residue of vomit, dead fish and seaweed. As he washed himself in the fresh water, he happened to notice his reflection in a still pool. Who was that horrible creature? He looked up and saw a child staring at him on the beach. The child started to cry and ran away.

Then he heard a voice. "Jonah!" His Boss. The word of the Lord came to Jonah a second time.

The command was the same: Go to Nineveh. No way Jonah was going to disobey again. He had a good twenty-day walk ahead of him. He had better get started.

Jonah was in the belly of a fish because of disobedience, rebellion and faithlessness. He did not deserve a second chance. I will tell you a secret: Jonah did not deserve his first chance, either. None of us deserve to serve in God's Kingdom. None of us are worthy servants.

All our first and second (and often many more) chances are by grace. The spiritual war today begins in each one of us. First, we discover that God forgives us. That He still loves us. Then He invites us to be His ambassadors.

For Reflection

Is there somewhere God is calling you to go?
Where? Maybe the call is to your neighborhood.
Can you start there? When will you go?

One Choice, a Lifetime of Consequences

By faith Moses, when he was grown up, refused to be called the son of Pharaoh's daughter, choosing rather to be mistreated with the people of God.

Hebrews 11:24–25

He thought it was better to suffer for the sake of Christ than to own the treasures of Egypt.

Hebrews 11:26 NLT

Moses is turning eighty—a natural time for reflection as he assumes he is near the end of his life.

What did Moses think about as he led a flock of sheep through the wilderness seeking the next pasture or watering hole? Did he recall the miracle of his birth? Did he long for the comforts of palace life? Did he regret the last forty "wasted" years spent in the land of Midian far away from his people, powerless to do anything to alleviate their suffering?

At one time Moses was on top of the world. He had attended the most prestigious university of his day. He was wealthy and wore the best clothing. He had servants and knew all the right people. He wielded genuine power. Everything about his situation and his future was positive.

He threw it all away because he chose to identify with the persecuted rather than the persecutors. Moses saw one Hebrew being beaten, and he killed the oppressor. When Pharaoh learned of this, Moses had to run for his life. That fit of anger was why he became a refugee in Midian.

During his second four decades, Moses must have reflected on that life-defining moment. Surely as a boy and young man Moses knew something about his heritage. He probably had occasional contact with his parents. Maybe clandestine talks with his older brother Aaron and his sister, Miriam?

He had to have understood that his kin were slaves. Hebrews were everywhere. He might avoid them in the palace, but he could not miss them when he traveled throughout Egypt and observed how hard they were forced to work (see Exodus 2:11). One fateful day he decided to go visit his people. That is when Moses made *the choice* that changed his life.

We know Moses made a conscious decision to punish the man who was abusing "one of his people." He looked around to make sure no one was watching. With his military training, it was not hard to kill the persecutor. The problem was disposal of the body. The only option was to bury it quickly in the sand. That is not the best burial ground, but it was all the Prince of Egypt had available.

Some might wonder if Moses ever considered what he might have accomplished had he stayed in Pharaoh's palace. Rather than try to be a hero, given his political clout, might he have done more for the Hebrews than was accomplished by eliminating a single persecutor? No, Moses chose the right path, but he employed a carnal method. Nothing is accomplished by responding to injustice with violence.

As the writer of the Epistle to the Hebrews noted: Moses "chose to share the oppression of God's people instead of enjoying the fleeting pleasures of sin. He thought it was better to suffer for the sake of Christ than to own the treasures of Egypt" (Hebrews 11:25–26 NLT).

Already the laws of Christ were written on Moses' heart. No, he did not know about Jesus specifically—that would come much later. But he acted on principle. Looking at the situation—a nation in slavery to a nation of oppressors—the picture was clear. How could he continue living in unbridled luxury with, no doubt, the immorality that accompanied such a life? He could not! Moses knew something was wrong. The principle of Christ was working in his life.

When we recognize principles of justice, they provide direction on how to evaluate the actions of politicians and cultural influencers. They give us the direction we need to counter evil. Moses had to act when he recognized injustice.

Some may protest that we cannot expect people to act on principle if they do not know the laws of God. Well, Moses did not know the laws of God—they would be revealed on Mount Sinai many years later. Moses, however, knew what was right. Scripture says that everyone does. Just examine the first chapter of Romans. Anyone can make right choices based on principle even if they have never heard the Gospel.

For Reflection

What troubles you when you think about standing up against injustice? Are you willing to identify with your Christian brothers and sisters who suffer for following Christ? What might that mean for your dreams and plans?

Encounter with Fire

The angel of the LORD appeared to him in a flame of fire out of the midst of a bush. He looked, and behold, the bush was burning, yet it was not consumed.

Exodus 3:2

Year after year rolled by with no evidence that God paid any attention to Moses or the children of Israel. The people of Israel cried out to God for help—there were no other options. But heaven was silent. The future seemed exceedingly bleak. Day after day they were abused. People lived, worked as slaves and died. They passed along the stories of the patriarchs to their children. But after decades, then hundreds of years, those

107

tales began to sound like the myth of Santa Claus. Their family stories did not bring them one step closer to freedom.

Moses was not suffering as his countrymen were. He was herding sheep. He had to wonder how he had moved from a lofty position as a prince in the Egyptian royal family to a lowly shepherd. These were not even his animals. Did he wonder: *Is this my reward for acting on principle?* He had risked everything to address injustice. Probably he had expected . . . just what had Moses expected? That he would lead a revolt? That he would organize the slaves and they would rise up against their tormentors, break free from their bondage and escape to freedom?

Do not minimize the bleakness of this situation. After forty years in the wilderness, Moses may have looked back on his life and thought, *What a waste!* If that was what Moses thought, he was nearing the time when God could use him.

Forty years earlier, when Moses was young and strong, he was eager to do something. Now he was just old. Eighty is a good age to retire from shepherding. Leave the work to a younger generation. Marry off the kids, enjoy the grandkids and die in your sleep. But rather than sit at home, Moses continued leading a herd of sheep and goats around a mountain— one of many in the region. There was nothing that would set it apart from dozens of other hills and peaks. That is, until God appeared.

How does God get someone's attention? A burning bush that is not consumed will certainly do the job. Moses said,

"I will turn aside to see this great sight, why the bush is not burned" (Exodus 3:3). A more contemporary translation might be, "Finally, some excitement! These sheep aren't going anywhere. Let's check this out!"

David writes that God "made known his ways to Moses" (Psalm 103:7). That began on the holy mountain when God introduced Himself. It was the start of a unique relationship. No one, until the disciples met Jesus, had experienced anything approaching the closeness Moses had with God. It lasted for forty years and matured into an intimacy that was almost terrifying. Scripture says Moses met with God face-to-face "as a man speaks to his friend" (Exodus 33:11).

Do any of us really desire such closeness with God? For most people the answer probably is no! Such a relationship is frightening and costly; however, it is an adventure that no one should miss. Moses' intimacy with God may have been unique in the Old Testament, but in the New Testament, Jesus revealed that He was making it possible for *everyone* to know God. He took on flesh so that people could talk with Him, touch Him and learn what was on His heart.

The apostle Paul prayed that he might "know [Christ] and the power of his resurrection, and may share his sufferings" (Philippians 3:10). That was the power of the encounter Moses had. One moment there was no hope, then despair turned into glorious promise. There was resurrection!

We can have the same kind of close encounter today, and we do not need a burning bush experience.

For Reflection

How much do you really want to know God—to talk with Him, to know His heart? What frightens you about that prospect? What excites you?

3

An Impossible Assignment

Then the LORD said, "I have surely seen the affliction of my people. . . . Come, I will send you to Pharaoh that you may bring my people, the children of Israel, out of Egypt."

Exodus 3:7, 10

Moses probably thought that his decision to identify with God's people was meaningless.

Why make a principled stand, risking his life, if God turned His back and ignored the situation? But God had not turned His back.

We tend to forget that God's time is not our time. A thousand years for us are like a day in His sight or like a watch in the night (see Psalm 90:4). That is only three hours if you are counting. So in God's chronology not even one day had passed since Joseph had led his family to safety in Egypt.

If Moses knew about God's timing, it was likely not very comforting. Four hundred years is a long time for humans. So is forty years. Moses needed something concrete. He got it at the burning bush. Immediately after God introduced Himself to Moses as "the God of your father [interesting that God begins with Moses' own father], the God of Abraham, the God of Isaac, and the God of Jacob" (Exodus 3:6), He got right to the point. Read carefully:

> I have *surely seen* the affliction of *my people* who are in Egypt and have heard their cry because of their taskmasters. I *know* their sufferings, and I have come down to *deliver* them out of the hand of the Egyptians and *to bring them* up out of that land to a good and broad land, a land flowing with milk and honey.
>
> Exodus 3:7–8, emphasis added

God understood the condition of His people. He knew they were suffering. He planned to rescue them and bring them out of Egypt to a new land, a good country, a place filled with tasty and nourishing food and drink.

Then, God asked Moses to be His partner. Let's paraphrase what God said: "Guess what, Moses? Today is your lucky day! You are the answer to many prayers. You are going to rescue my people from slavery and lead them out of Egypt."

Moses replies, "Who me? You have got to be kidding!" Have you ever felt that way?

Moses' reaction makes perfect sense. "Who am I that I should go to Pharaoh and bring the children of Israel out of Egypt?" (Exodus 3:11). Remember, Moses was ready to retire. You cannot start your life's work at age eighty. Or can you?

Forty years earlier, Moses might have said, "Yes, God. I am Your man. I can get right into Pharaoh's court, no problem. I've got the language, the training and all the skills You need. Pharaoh will have to listen to me. I have plans—I can organize the people, and if the Egyptian army tries to stop us, I know their tactics so we can thwart them. Just leave everything to me!"

Forty years in the wilderness had stripped Moses of that hubris. His language skills were rusty. He had not kept up with all the news of Egypt. He was out of touch with the latest palace politics. He had no internet connection, and therefore no email contact with friends and family. Forty years earlier, he was the man. Now it would be a disaster. *Which means God had Moses right where He wanted him.*

If you read the Bible, you realize that God loves to hand out impossible assignments. We have already seen it with David, Elijah and Jonah. One crazy, impossible job after another. Why? Because these assignments can never be accomplished by human effort. *God must step in and do the impossible, and He will get the glory.*

Jesus wants us to take the Gospel all over the world, to make disciples of every tribe and nation (see Matthew 28:19). Each of us is called to play an important part. One family goes to Africa, another couple to the Middle East, while a team heads into the jungles of the Amazon. Meanwhile, others fund the missions, feed the poor, build hospitals for the sick, tackle the problem of AIDS, feed and house the homeless, educate children mired in poverty and do many other good works. None of this is accomplished without divine help.

Moses had an impossible task. He could not possibly succeed unless God acted. And God was not going to leave Moses without the resources he needed.

God's answer to Moses' question was simple: "I will be with you" (verse 12).

For Reflection

How will God get the glory when your impossible assignment is fulfilled? What resources has He given you? If you feel inadequate, tell Him right now and ask Him to provide what you will need.

4

What's in a Name?

Then Moses said to God, "If I come to the people of Israel and say to them, 'The God of your fathers has sent me to you,' and they ask me, 'What is his name?' what shall I say to them?"

Exodus 3:13

Moses knew the culture of Egypt. He realized that he could not speak on his own authority. He understood the awesome powers of Pharaoh, the authority of the priests in the Egyptian temples and the intimidation of the whips of Israel's slave masters. The Hebrews needed more than just a nice story about Abraham that had been told by Grandpa around the campfire.

For centuries the people of Israel had known about the God who appeared to their forefathers—a God with no name.

Egypt was populated by deities with names: Isis, the goddess of magic and secrets; Osiris, who supposedly granted life through the river Nile. There was the frog goddess and the earth god, the god of beetles, and the god of flies. Moses needed to speak for more than an unnamed deity.

If you detect a pattern in the list of Egyptian deities, you should. Soon the God who spoke to Moses will confront each of the Egyptian gods through a different plague. He will demonstrate that He is greater than Pharaoh's magicians and the mighty Nile, that He rules over deities represented by frogs and gnats and flies and beetles as well as the gods of livestock and weather and trees. Even the great sun god Ra will be obliterated by darkness. Finally, the tenth and last plague will expose the god Bloed, touching every household in Egypt and demonstrating that Bloed has no ability to save. Israel meanwhile will be saved by the blood of lambs.

God provides two answers to Moses' question. First, He says, "I am who I am" or "I am the One who is" or "I will be what I will be." *Yahweh* is the Hebrew word that means "I am." Moses is instructed to tell Israel "I AM has sent me to you" (Exodus 3:14). With this name, God reveals that He is self-existent, uncreated and undefined by any other.

This is a breakthrough concept. God, the eternal Spirit who spoke into existence the universe out of nothing, who crafted the earth and then molded man and breathed life into him—He has now formally introduced Himself.

God provides a second answer to Moses' question:

"Say this to the people of Israel: 'The LORD, the God of your fathers, the God of Abraham, the God of Isaac, and the God of Jacob, has sent me to you.' This is my name forever, and thus I am to be remembered throughout all generations."

Exodus 3:15

God is the great I AM, Creator of all things. He is also a personal deity—the God of your fathers, and yes, Moses, your God! God says He is not just the God of spiritual giants like Abraham, Isaac and Jacob. He is also the God of every Hebrew suffering in slavery. He is the God of every person living today in bondage to sin. He is a personal God.

Note we said *personal*, not *private*. This is the God who will lead the people of Israel to freedom. He will liberate a nation. He will rescue every individual in that nation.

A dialogue follows. One thing to savor about many of the Old Testament heroes is how they interact with God. They do not just talk. They argue, debate, negotiate, disagree, explore options and reach understandings. These are not sound-bite chats, though, because of space considerations, we are pretty sure the Bible provides only highlights of most conversations.

From the very start of this relationship, Moses was not just listening for instructions. He was fully engaged, proposing alternatives and explaining why he was not the right person for the job. God patiently answered every objection. I AM lost patience only when Moses told Him, "Send someone else" (Exodus 4:13).

How typical! Today many men would answer God's call with, "Here I am, Lord! Send my sister." (There are far more women on the mission field than men. Makes us wonder how many Christian men have ignored God's call.) God answered Moses by telling him that his brother would help him, and that was the end of this discussion; however, their talks continued over the next forty years. A deep intimacy grew between them to the point that we can safely say that Moses had a closer relationship with God than anyone else prior to the arrival of Jesus.

Today, anyone can have the same closeness with almighty God that Moses enjoyed.

For Reflection

*What do the two names that God revealed to
Moses say to you about who God is?*

5

The Necessary Tools

Then Moses answered, "But behold, they will not believe me
or listen to my voice, for they will say, 'The LORD did not
appear to you.'"

Exodus 4:1

Moses said to the LORD, "Oh, my Lord, I am not eloquent."

Exodus 4:10

But he said, "Oh, my Lord, please send someone else."

Exodus 4:13

What does this initial conversation between I AM and Moses
covering one-and-a-half chapters of Exodus consist of?

Notice that Moses was not concerned about things we tend to bring up. He did not protest, "God, that is not safe. If I go to Pharaoh, he will kill me." While that was a legitimate concern, Moses never mentioned it.

Or Moses could have said, "What about my finances? What is the budget? It will not be cheap to rescue two million people. Are you going to pay me, or will I have to raise the money? That will take time." No, Moses seemed confident that God would provide for his financial and material needs.

It is natural when we sense God's call to mission to ask many practical questions. Practical details were not covered in Moses' discussion with God. Two important areas were covered. God introduced Himself, and He revealed compassion for His suffering people. *Mission begins with these two vital ingredients: knowing God and knowing God's heart for people.* When we understand these two things, we are on the right path.

God did provide a few instructions. He told Moses first to go to the elders of Israel, and He told Moses what to say in that meeting. Together, Moses and the elders were to go to Pharaoh. Again, God provided the script Moses would deliver.

Regarding the conversation with the Hebrew elders, Moses anticipated that his authority would be challenged. "The LORD did not appear to you," the Hebrews would say. God provided Moses with several signs of authority. One sign would be that the staff he carried, when thrown on the ground, would become a snake. Pick it up by the tail, and it would become a staff again. A second sign was that Moses would put his hand in his cloak. When he removed it, the hand would be leprous like snow. When he repeated the move, the hand would be restored. A third sign was that he was to take some water from the Nile and pour it on the ground. When he did that, it would turn to blood.

Pretty powerful tools, don't you think? Moses had everything he needed—but he did not see it that way. He protested, "Oh, my Lord, I am not eloquent, either in the past or since you have spoken to your servant, but I am slow of speech and of tongue" (verse 10). We do not know the exact problem. Some have speculated that Moses stuttered. Probably he felt insecure about the assignment. Any one of us in that situation would have felt anxious.

Patiently God addressed the concern. "Who has made man's mouth? Who makes him mute, or deaf, or seeing, or blind? Is it not I, the LORD? Now therefore go, and I will be with your mouth and teach you what you shall speak" (verses 11–12). Those are powerful words. *This should provide us with the assurance that what God requires of us, He will provide.* He is the Creator. He will not give us an impossible assignment and then leave us without the tools to accomplish the job.

So Moses ran out of excuses. All he could sputter was, "Lord, please send someone else." That is when God became angry. Yet even here, we observe Yahweh's compassion. God offered Moses a partner, his brother Aaron, a man who was articulate. Moses just had to tell Aaron what to say, and he would speak for Moses.

Moses indeed relied on Aaron early in the mission. You see it the next few chapters of Exodus. Aaron stood next to Moses and spoke to the elders, and he spoke for Moses to Pharaoh. Notice, however, that after the third plague, we no longer hear from Aaron. Moses spoke directly to Pharaoh and the people. By the end of his life, as we read his sermons in Deuteronomy, we recognize that Moses was a powerful and eloquent speaker. All this goes to demonstrate that God had the right man with the right tools for the job.

Do not fear! You can trust God to provide exactly what you need to fulfill His mission.

For Reflection

As you consider God's mission for your life, where do you feel inadequate? Talk to God about this, and then listen for His answer. How has He provided what you need?

6

Impact on Family

So Moses took his wife and his sons . . . and went back to the land of Egypt.

Exodus 4:20

Moses obeyed God—he did not really have a choice. That is the reality of a mandate from the Ruler of the universe. But it was not only his life that changed. Moses had a wife, children and a father-in-law who was known as the priest of Midian (see Exodus 2:16).

The story of Moses' entry into a family is touching. Following his flight from Egypt, feeling relatively safe in the midst of the desert, he sat down by a well. Seven young women showed up and began to water their father's flock. Moses must have enjoyed watching these sisters care for the sheep. Did he notice one in particular—Zipporah, the woman he would eventually marry?

Then trouble arrived. The account in Exodus lacks detail. It simply says, "The shepherds came and drove them away, but Moses stood up and saved them, and watered their flock" (Exodus 2:17). Remember that Moses detested bullies—that is what those shepherds were. As when he saw the abusive Egyptian beating his countryman, Moses could not ignore oppression. He had to act. These rough-and-tumble shepherds were no match for a battle-tested Moses. As a result, he gained something he very much needed—a family.

The family was headed by a priest called Reuel (see Exodus 2:18). He was better known as Jethro. We do not know much about his faith. Was he a priest of the true living God? Probably not. But he was the religious leader of his tribe and that was where God placed Moses for his protection. Moses could not survive alone for forty years. He needed to do some meaningful work. He needed a family with whom he could rest, enjoy meals and talk with an older man. Jethro was a wise father-in-law who would one day help Moses organize the leadership structure of the Israelites.

Moses also helped solve a problem for Jethro. The priest needed to find husbands for his daughters, and clearly Moses was a good choice for Zipporah.

What kind of marriage was it? Happy? Maybe not. Did the young woman know much about her husband? Obviously, he was well educated. Zipporah likely was illiterate. Did Moses reveal details about his birth, his life in Pharaoh's court, or that he was wanted on charges of murder? It is doubtful that Moses had many deep and meaningful conversations with his wife.

So, Moses returned from the mountain where he had his encounter with the burning bush. For the first time in decades, he had a purpose in life. There was a job to do and no time to waste. Arriving home, he quickly pushed the sheep into their pen and went to talk with Jethro.

"Please let me go back to my brothers in Egypt to see whether they are still alive" (Exodus 4:18). That is not exactly the full story, but it is plausible. He has not seen Aaron or Miriam for forty years. His father-in-law gives his blessing: "Go in peace."

Now, how to tell his wife and sons, Gershom and Eliezer. This was trickier. God provides a little more information: "Go back to Egypt, for all the men who were seeking your life are dead" (verse 19). That was good to know. The statute of limitations had run out. It was safe for his family to travel there with him; therefore, Moses packed the family donkey and moved to his boyhood home.

It was not an easy trip. There are three verses that describe a traumatic event at a hotel along the way. Details are sketchy. It says the Lord met Moses and "sought to put him to death" (Exodus 4:24). It must have been a terrifying moment for Zipporah. She saved her husband's life by performing an emergency circumcision on their son, probably Gershom. If the boy was going to be part of God's chosen people, this was a necessary step.

A decision to follow the call of God always affects others. It is not unusual for parents to worry about a daughter headed to the mission field. A transfer to a new job can uproot a wife and the children who may or may not support the move. What if family does not agree with the head of household? The husband and wife might fight over the decision. This is often a hidden element of spiritual conflict.

Regardless of the dynamics at home, Moses had no choice but to follow God's instructions. It is the same for us. Christian marriage is a three-way relationship with Christ as the head. The husband is to love his wife and children with understanding just as Christ loves him. Ultimately, however, the call of God must be heeded.

For Reflection

God has placed you in a family. Think about how God has used them in your personal and spiritual development. Are they supportive of your first call to obey God? If not, what can you do today to improve the situation?

The Root Problem

The people of Israel did what was evil in the sight of the LORD, and the LORD gave them into the hand of Midian seven years.

Judges 6:1

Let's begin by looking at Gideon's circumstances. When the angel of the Lord found him, he was beating out wheat. Not in the open on a threshing floor where the wind would carry away the chaff, but in a winepress. He should have been crushing grapes after a great harvest and celebrating with the community; instead, he was hiding his pitiful stash of grain from the Midianites.

This was not the good life in the Promised Land.

God had delivered Israel to the Midianites for seven years. We should not miss the irony here because these invaders have a strong link to the Israelites. It goes back all the way to Abraham who, after the death of Sarah, married Keturah who bore him six sons. One of them was Midian. Abraham gave gifts to Midian and his brothers and sent them away to the east, separating them from Isaac who inherited Abraham's estate.

Midian moved into what is now Saudi Arabia, settling in an area east of the Gulf of Aqabah. The Midianites were a nomadic people, a necessity given the rugged desert conditions. Moving around on their camels, they respected no boundaries and likely roamed a wide area looking for water and trade and trouble. It is no surprise that a caravan of Midianite traders purchased a teenage boy from his eleven jealous brothers and took him to Egypt where they made a nice little profit selling him to Potiphar (see Genesis 39). These nomads were unwitting agents of God's plan to save Israel.

A few hundred years later, Moses fled Egypt and Pharaoh's anger and settled in the land of Midian. The priest of Midian provided Moses a family for forty years.

We meet the Midianites again in Numbers when they harassed the Israelites, and God told Moses to "harass the Midianites and strike them down" (Numbers 25:17). Before entering the Promised Land, Israel went to war with Midian and killed every male in their army along with their five kings and Balaam, the seer who had been hired to curse the Israelites.

Now, two hundred years later, Midian is back. The nomads covet the prosperity of Israel. Since God's people have violated their covenant, God allows them to be overrun and oppressed. The Hebrews no longer enjoy their homes and vineyards and pastures full of sheep and cattle. They hide in the mountains, in caves and in dens. Rather than thriving, they barely survive. They are imprisoned by fear.

The fear is real, but is Midian really the problem? Sure, the devastation that the Midian horde leaves behind is compared to a plague of locusts that devours all plant life and leaves Israel in desperate straits; however, Moses preached that if Israel did not obey all God commanded, a host of curses would crush them (see Deuteronomy 28).

Here are just a few specifics:

- The Lord will cause you to be defeated before your enemies.
- You shall build a house, but you shall not dwell in it.
- You shall plant a vineyard, but you shall not enjoy its fruit.
- Your ox shall be slaughtered before your eyes, but you shall not eat any of it.
- Your sheep shall be given to your enemies, but there shall be no one to help you.
- A nation that you have not known shall eat up the fruit of your ground.

In case they missed the point, Moses provides this summary: "All these curses shall come upon you and pursue you and overtake you . . . because you did not obey the voice of the LORD your God" (Deuteronomy 28:45–46). To anyone who is willing to pay attention and look up the words Moses spoke, the core problem is obvious.

Unfortunately, we fail to recognize the root cause of many problems we face today. Did Gideon understand the situation? Did he even consider that God wanted to get his and his nation's attention? Disasters should force us to go to God, repent and discover what He may be revealing to us.

Who will recognize the root problems today? Someone needs to step up and lead God's people to victory. Like Gideon, any one of us could be a candidate if we are listening for His call and are willing to obey when He tells us to go.

For Reflection

What ongoing problems does the culture present today?
Be specific. Ask the why questions and dig down to the
root cause. Then ask, How is God inviting you to pray?

2

We Cry Out—God Answers

When the people of Israel cried out to the LORD . . . the LORD sent a prophet to the people of Israel.

Judges 6:7–8

Finally, the people pray! Why does it take them seven years to cry out for help?

Maybe because Israel thought they could solve the problem of Midian themselves. Perhaps they mounted a defense of their lands but were overrun. Then maybe they tried praying to their idols. Possibly the first year or two they thought this was just a momentary blip. They believed that they could wait this out, plant new crops and next year everything would be fine.

Did anyone realize that this was a curse?

Well, at least they prayed. That is the first sign of hope. Praying would remind them that God had rescued them before; therefore, maybe He would rescue them again. That is faith. But first, God has a word for the people. The answer to their prayers started with a prophet sent by God.

This prophet is not named. The messenger is not important, while the message is vital. Truth must be proclaimed.

The sermon is short but powerful. A nice three-point outline:

One, you have forgotten your history.

Two, you have forgotten your God.

Three, you have not listened to God.

The application is also clear: Remember the God who rescued you from Egypt and gave you this land. Repent, return to God and obey His law as revealed to Moses at Mount Sinai.

Grab your Bibles. Read Genesis, Exodus, Leviticus, Numbers and Deuteronomy. When we cry out to God, we must ask, "What is God's message today?" We can find it in Father's Book. There is no other solution but the Word of God.

I am not going to waste my time with psychologists and all the intellectuals who use an enormous amount of words to say nothing. I am certainly not putting my trust in politicians who will promise anything to get elected. The only thing that might change is that you will have an empty wallet. Certainly, your concerns and worries remain.

God gives the Word. When people in the Bible get into trouble, God speaks a word. When we go into the world with the Word, we are incredibly strong. That is why, regardless of where I have gone in the world, I have carried Scripture. As a young Christian, I joined the Pocket Testament League. As a member, I pledged to always carry at least a New Testament with me wherever I went. Many seeds were sown with those Scripture passages.

Even in the Muslim world, they want the Word of God— they beg for it. When I was in Lebanon during their civil war, I practiced what I call checkpoint evangelism. It was not unusual to have to pass through a dozen checkpoints in a day while moving between Muslim and Christian sectors. I always offered the soldiers Bibles. Muslims often said they only wanted "the Jesus Bible," meaning the New Testament, what they call the *Injil*. They eagerly took it. As we drove away, I often saw them opening and reading the Word.

Unfortunately, too many Christians do not spend enough time in Father's Book. Is it really necessary that we find ourselves in deep trouble before we open the Word? Well, if it takes a disaster or crisis to get someone to read Scripture, God uses that.

Here is a suggestion: Why not get to know the Lord when times are good? Any time is a good time to commit our lives to God's service. God still speaks today. He does not give up because He has provided a solution in and through Jesus Christ. The fact is that this is the source of our hope. People should see that hope in us and want to ask us about it when we are in crisis.

In Lebanon, people often asked me, "Andrew, do you see a future for us? Do you have a word from God?" The answer is a resounding *yes*. It is right there in the Bible.

God's word to us is *remember*. Remember how God brought the Israelites out of Egypt. Remember all the times the people cried out to God and repented of their idolatry, and He rescued them. Remember that God so loved the world that He sent His only beloved son Jesus who took our sins on Himself on the cross.

Refresh your memory!

For Reflection

Review your plan for reading the Bible. Do you need to make an adjustment? Maybe allow a little more time for daily reading. God has a message for you in His Word.

3

God Is with You

Now the angel of the LORD came and sat under the terebinth at Ophrah. . . . And the angel of the LORD appeared to him and said to him, "The LORD is with you, O mighty man of valor."

Judges 6:11–12

Gideon hides. He is a secret believer. He threshes wheat in a winepress, a pit that was carved out of rocky ground. It probably provided him with a decent hiding place where he could provide a little grain for his family. He might be hiding successfully from the Midianites, but he is not hiding from God. An angel comes to him with a very specific message.

God's word to Gideon has two parts.

The *first revelation* is "the LORD is with you." Really? Gideon did not believe God was with Israel, much less with him personally. No doubt he had heard the prophet's message. He had reminded himself of the history God had with this people. He was ready to turn his back on Baal and Asherah—they were the gods his father worshiped. But he had no personal relationship with Yahweh.

That was about to change. God reveals, "I am with you." *What a shocking concept! God was with Abraham, Moses and Joshua. But me? I am a nobody. God does not even know I exist. Here I am trying to eke out a living without attracting attention of the invaders.*

Ever felt that way? Talk about a poor self-image. Gideon could not slink much lower in his thinking. This truth makes the *second revelation* even more shocking: "O mighty man of valor."

Gideon must think that God has him confused with someone else. What about that great archer in the tribe of Ephraim? Or maybe Joachim who lives a few doors down—he is a body builder, and no one can pin him in a wrestling match. That explains it; the angel went to the wrong address. This must be a mistake.

Hear Gideon's protest: "How can I save Israel? Behold, my clan is the weakest in Manasseh, and I am the least in my father's house" (verse 15). How sad that Gideon only understands his miserable condition, his helplessness, his bondage. *Woe is me,* he thinks. He is steeped in fear.

Someone with courage needs to step up and confront the persecutors. But who? Gideon certainly does not volunteer. That is a good thing. If we try and manufacture courage, we are almost certain to fail. When thinking about a threat, we might write a speech in our minds telling off the bully. We imagine everyone cheering our powerful words. We visualize rising up, charging the enemy and beating him until his face is black and blue. We might even dream of the hero's parade that would follow. Those fantasies melt away when we actually face our foe.

We need courage that will persevere in battle. That is what God provides to Gideon. You are the man! You are a mighty warrior!

God is prepared to make a new beginning with anybody who is available, even the least of the least. We can have confidence when He calls us because He says, "I am with you."

Looking at Gideon's circumstances after the angel speaks, nothing changed. The Midianites were still roaming the land creating havoc. Yet everything changed because God arrived. He called Gideon, and that meant He was with Gideon.

Looking at your circumstances—whether cultural or political, a family crisis or a health pandemic—if you feel the situation is helpless, you are looking in the wrong direction. God is here. He is calling us. He is calling you, and that means He is with you and will equip you with everything you need for battle.

Here is what Jesus says: "Behold, I am with you always, to the end of the age" (Matthew 28:20). That is the starting point we need to prepare for the spiritual fight.

For Reflection

Looking at the circumstances around you right now, do you sense that God is with you? If not, why? Spend some time meditating on the words of Jesus, "I am with you always."

4

So Many Questions

Gideon said to him, "Please, my lord, if the LORD is with us, why then has all this happened to us?"

Judges 6:13

I think Gideon gets a bad rap. He has been charged with lacking faith because of his questions, then laying out the fleece so God can confirm his mission. The writer of Hebrews, however, lists Gideon as one of the heroes of the faith "who through faith conquered kingdoms" (Hebrews 11:32).

It is true, Gideon has many questions. God has said, "You are a mighty man of valor" and "The Lord is with you." What more does Gideon need to know? Where is Gideon's faith?

Here is an important truth for us to remember: Faith depends on a relationship, not a religion. God has no problem with Gideon's questions. In fact, He welcomes them.

Abraham questioned God about His promise to give Abraham's descendants the land of Canaan. Moses questioned how God could use him when he struggled with public speaking. Before Jesus ascended, His disciples asked if now they were going to see the kingdom restored to Israel. Paul questioned God about the thorn in his flesh.

Norman Grubb, who was the leader of Worldwide Evangelization Crusade, once said: "God does not mind if you have a quarrel with him as long as you give in at the end."[1]

Honest questions bring an honest response from God. Consider the questions Gideon asks:

- If the Lord is with us, why then has all this happened to us?
- Where are all God's wonderful deeds that our fathers recounted to us, saying, "Did not the Lord bring us up from Egypt?"
- Now the Lord has forsaken us and given us into the hand of Midian.

The last one is not a formal question, but you can hear it: If God is with me, with us, why are we being persecuted? What has gone wrong? These are good questions. The facts on the ground do not seem to demonstrate that God was really with them.

I am sure Gideon had heard stories. His grandparents had told him about Deborah and Barak. He knew about the miracles, but he had never seen any himself.

For answers, we need to go back to the Word of God. The prophet told the people that God had delivered them from Egypt and all who oppressed them. The issue: "You have not obeyed my voice." God's diagnosis could not be plainer. The problem was not with God. Look within. Look at the nation's practices. Compare that to the revealed Word of God. Gideon, do you recognize the problem?

Jesus says, "I am with you always." You protest: We do not see evidence that Jesus is with us. Perhaps the reason is that we do not fulfill God's conditions. Jesus says, "Go, make disciples." Go, and I am with you. Have we obeyed His command?

We are invited to ask hard questions. I have a few, such as these:

If God is with us, where is the unity of the Church that Jesus prayed for in John 17?

We are told to pray for the peace of Jerusalem. Why is there no peace in Israel, in Jerusalem? All we see in the news from Jerusalem and Israel is conflict.

Why is there the challenge from Islam? Why are most terrorists Muslim? Good questions. We need to understand the conflict with Islam. Maybe we should also ask why we do not reach out to them?

Let's get more personal and look at our culture. Why are so many marriages and families falling apart? Even Christian families. Why are there so many abortions? Why is there so much violence in the streets? Why are not more Christians standing up against evil? Why is there so much division in our politics?

These questions ought to bring us to tears. They should produce compassion as we pray. We cannot be God's warriors in this world without compassion. That empathy will emerge as we take our problems, our questions, the news we see on television or in newspapers or on the internet and turn them into prayer.

One more point. Later on, again out of his relationship, Gideon uses the fleece test to confirm God's promise of deliverance. This extra validation is just what Gideon needs to move forward. The fleece is an act of faith because it comes out of his relationship with God. In this relationship there is no fear. Gideon is not afraid to ask. That is the privilege we have of abiding in Christ.

For Reflection

What issues in the culture produce tears in you? What questions do you want to ask of God? Where do you need discernment for the call you sense on your life?

5

God's Answer to Gideon's Questions

And the LORD turned to him and said, "Go in this might of yours and save Israel from the hand of Midian; do not I send you?"

Judges 6:14

The answer to all of Gideon's questions is *go*!

There is a time to reflect, discuss and pray. Then it is time for *action*. Gideon is not being called to answer hard questions. He is not ensconced in a seminary, writing a Ph.D. dissertation on Israel's frequent lapses into idolatry. There is no discussion

143

of how to solve the problem of Midian. Gideon is being commissioned. He is being told to get off the bench and get in the game. He is no longer third string, junior varsity. He is moving onto the varsity starting lineup in a critical position.

It is great to get this promotion. But what is the strategy? What play is Gideon supposed to run? He is clueless until God gives directions. Those instructions will surprise everyone—the opponents as well as the Israelites. But let's not rush too quickly into battle. First, Gideon must understand who is in charge, which gets to the heart of Gideon's questions. Where is this great power of God that we have heard so much about? Those miracles in Egypt and the wilderness—those were centuries ago. Those great stories I heard as a boy about the walls of Jericho falling down and the defeat of a dozen kings and the conquest of this land. Those are great tales. But what has God done for us recently? We do not see it.

God tells Gideon, "Go in this might of yours and save Israel." Wait a minute! What might? Gideon has no strength to save himself, much less an entire nation. God is sending Gideon, but with what resources? How about a few automatic weapons to mow down the Midianites? That would at least even the playing field.

No, God has already answered the question with these words: "The LORD is with you" (verse 12). Gideon is to go, and along the way God will provide all the instructions and resources he needs.

It is the same when God calls us into battle today. Cling to the final words Jesus spoke to His disciples in Matthew's gospel: "I am with you always, to the end of the age" (Matthew 28:20). Here is the perfect antidote for fear. What greater confidence does anyone need?

An argument follows because Gideon cannot yet see the big picture. He is focused on his abilities and resources that are negligible. How can he possibly save Israel? His clan is the weakest of the tribe. He is the least of the least. Gideon concentrates on facts and logic. How does God answer that?

God: "But I will be with you."

There it is again. Gideon, that is all you need to know—God is with you. This is the most wonderful information God can give any human being. Forget the facts. Ignore the human evidence. Forget the logic.

God provides an additional detail: "You shall strike the Midianites as one man."

Think about that. One man versus 120,000 soldiers. Is this some kind of video game where the player at the controls mows down thousands of demons? Not at all. There is no magic joystick. All you need to know is that God is with you, and His resources are unlimited. The odds have been evened out—actually, they are now in your favor. How can that be? Stay tuned for more details.

A few decades later, David will write a psalm that captures what Gideon cannot yet comprehend. "God shall arise, his enemies shall be scattered; and those who hate him shall flee before him" (Psalm 68:1).

It has always been that way. Gideon needs to study his history. What resources does he have? "The chariots of God are twice ten thousand, thousands upon thousands; the Lord is among them" (Psalm 68:17).

Do you see how the odds have completely changed? If only the Midianites knew—they would pack up their tents and flee back to the desert.

This is where courage begins. Humanly, it does not look doable. You cannot see God or His chariots. But if God says go, well, you go. By faith.

Gideon cannot grasp it. All he can think is, *I can't do this.*

God's answer is, "You are absolutely right. But I am with you. So you can!"

For Reflection

What resources do you have to go into battle in today's culture? Are they adequate for the battle? Why or why not? What resources does God provide you?

The Battle Begins at Home

And he said to him, "If now I have found favor in your eyes, then show me a sign that it is you who speak with me."

Judges 6:17

That night the LORD said to him, "Take your father's bull, and the second bull seven years old, and pull down the altar of Baal that your father has, and cut down the Asherah that is beside it and build an altar to the LORD your God."

Judges 6:25–26

Gideon did not have all the information we have today. His only Bible was the first five books of Moses. He had heard some stories. But up until then, he had not had an encounter with the living God. So, Gideon requested a sign.

With typical Middle Eastern hospitality, he prepared a meal. He slaughtered a young goat, and while the meat was roasting, he baked some bread, minus the yeast. When the feast was ready, Gideon put the meat in a basket and the broth in a pot and carried them out to the terebinth tree where the angel of God waited patiently.

The angel instructed Gideon to place the meat and bread on a rock, then to pour the broth over the food. Gideon was then to stand back. The angel stretched out his staff, touched the meat and there was an explosion. Fire erupted and consumed the meat and unleavened cakes. Then the angel vanished.

Who would not be shaken by such an experience? Immediately God spoke to Gideon. How? Was there an audible voice? Or did he hear the words in his mind? Regardless of how, divine words calmed his racing heart: "Peace be to you. Do not fear; you shall not die" (verse 23).

Gideon's next step was perfect. He built an altar to God and gave it a name: "The LORD is Peace" (verse 24). He probably started with the rock on which his offering was incinerated.

It is impossible to go into spiritual battle until you have had a personal encounter with the Lord. The proper response to any revelation from God is worship.

Your experience with God, however, will not remain private. Your recruitment into spiritual battle will affect your family. Usually sooner rather than later you will experience a situation in which you must decide if God is really first in your life. Or do your parents still have primary authority? Or your spouse? Your children?

God prepares Gideon for his big assignment against the Midian army. What better place to start transforming the nation than within Gideon's home. But it is dangerous. Gideon is instructed to tear down the family shrine. He is to take two bulls, pull down the Baal idol, cut down the Asherah pole and then in their place build an altar to the Lord and sacrifice one of the bulls on it.

This act took guts. Gideon was rejecting his father's faith. In that culture, you never challenged the authority of the patriarch. There were relatives, siblings, aunts and uncles who would never question Papa's beliefs. That is why Gideon felt he could not obey God's instructions in broad daylight. He recruited ten men, and in the dead of night carried out God's orders.

Gideon acted in secret. But at least he did it!

It is never enough to *think* we will change and put God first. At some point we must *act* on that intention. Those actions will likely offend others. In the family context, that may be the toughest test we will face. That is the tension of obeying the fifth commandment: Honor your father and your mother. *Gideon, aren't your actions violating God's law?*

In Luke 9, Jesus invited a potential disciple to "Follow me" (verse 59). The disciple was willing but said, "First, let me go and bury my father." Jesus' answer sounds terribly insensitive.

"Leave the dead to bury their own dead" (verse 60). Really? You mean this man cannot go to his father's funeral? How rude!

There may be another explanation. As long as that would-be-disciple's father was alive, that father remained the authority in the family. I wonder if the man was telling Jesus, "I will follow you after my father dies. Then I will be head of the family, and I can make that decision." Jesus explained that the priority was obedience to a greater authority. "As for you, go and proclaim the kingdom of God" (verse 60).

When Jesus said to let the dead bury the dead, perhaps He was stating that the man's father was dead spiritually. If so, then the first place to preach God's Kingdom was at home. To his father. That was the place to begin his ministry.

That is where Gideon started. What a frightening prospect. How would Papa respond? What would the relatives think?

Then he remembered: "The Lord is peace." Gideon obeyed, trusting that somehow God would protect him.

For Reflection

Is your family supportive of your first love? How can you lovingly put God first while heeding the command to honor your parents and love your wife or submit to your husband?

PART TWO

Fearless
FIGHTING

Introduction

The battle is on! Just look around you. Spiritual warfare is evident because God's sworn enemy has used the same tools for thousands of years—lies, stealing, killing and destruction. These are the defining marks of evil. They must be cast out of God's Kingdom.

Wherever God has called you into the conflict, expect intense resistance. The devil and his minions will do everything in their power to thwart your efforts. There will be setbacks. Failures. Even casualties. If we are not prepared, fear may cause us to run away.

Fear is Satan's preferred instrument. This is my favorite definition of fear: **F**alse **E**vidence **A**ppearing **R**eal. I recognize it almost every time I see a political ad. I hear it when someone lashes out against another political party by saying that they will ruin our nation. Many worry about climate change.

153

Others fear what will happen to our investments as the stock market rides a roller coaster. I particularly notice the fear many Christians have of Muslim immigrants—we have created an enemy image of Muslims. Just their appearance can challenge our safety and security.

On January 15, 1933, Dietrich Bonhoeffer preached a sermon entitled "Overcoming Fear" in Berlin:

> Fear secretly gnaws and eats away at all the ties that bind a person to God and to others, and when in a time of need that person reaches for those ties and clings to them, they break and the individual sinks back into himself or herself, helpless and despairing, while hell rejoices. . . . That is the final triumph of fear over us, that we are afraid to run away from it, and just let it enslave us.[1]

We do not need to fear if we know God has called us to this fight. Some time ago I was in a prayer meeting with George Verwer, the founder of Operation Mobilization. A brother prayed, "Lord, there are so many giants." George interrupted that prayer and shouted, "Praise the Lord. The greater the giant, the greater the fall!" I like that! We do not need to be afraid of the battle. The greater the opposition, the greater the victory.

Our five Old Testament warriors will now show us how to fight against the schemes of the devil, against the rulers, against the authorities, against the cosmic powers over this present darkness and against the spiritual forces of evil in the heavenly places (see Ephesians 6:11–12).

An Arsenal of Five Stones

Then he took his staff in his hand and chose five smooth stones from the brook and put them in his shepherd's pouch.

1 Samuel 17:40

He looked David over and saw that he was little more than a boy . . . and he despised him.

1 Samuel 17:42 NIV

What's that kid doing by the stream?

Picture the scene. Two armies facing each other across a valley. To engage, each army would have to rush down a steep slope, carefully step over stones and wade through the stream. Those rocks would be slippery, not the best footing for a soldier. That is one reason David needed his staff—to provide balance as he stepped over the rocks.

Goliath, lounging on a patch of grass on the other side of the brook, watched. During the forty days he had issued his challenge, no one had come down the slope into the valley. Now here was this boy, dressed in a simple short robe and wearing sandals. There was a pouch around his waist. He carried a staff. He was bending over and picking up stones.

There was no threat here. *Stupid kid! He's oblivious. Must be mentally challenged. Doesn't he realize there's a war going on? Isn't he afraid of the big bad giant? He should be. But he doesn't pay me any attention.*

The kid put the stones in his pouch, looked up at the giant and stared at him. The giant was perplexed. *Surely . . . no, it's not possible. They would never send a boy to do a man's job. Someone's playing a joke. Very funny, those Israelites.*

David stepped carefully on the slick rocks as he made his way across the creek. Then he stood and faced the Philistine on the enemy side of the stream. Goliath sat up. Was the boy going to throw a rock at him? Then he saw David reach into his pouch and pull out a sling.

Was Goliath taking David seriously? He was cautious. A trained fighter. He could not afford to let his guard down. This could be a trick. The boy could be a decoy to allow the real opponent to sneak around behind him.

So, we have reached the climax of our story. The giant finally realized that David really was Israel's champion. But first there is trash talk. Each side must have its say. We must clearly understand the stakes. Before a "shot" is fired, Goliath and David will each reveal their true character. Goliath shouted first. His booming, guttural voice carried and reverberated off the rocks.

"Am I a dog?" shouted Goliath. (In the margin of my Bible, I have written, "Yes!") "Am I a dog, that you come to me with sticks?" (1 Samuel 17:43). David was carrying one stick—his shepherd staff. Maybe the giant's vision was poor.

Then Goliath cursed David by his gods. When a man has lost control of a situation, he often resorts to swearing or intimidation: "Come to me, and I will give your flesh to the birds of the air and to the beasts of the field" (verse 44).

Either the giant was very cocky, or he covered up his anxiety with strong words that he believed would instill fear in his opponent. Or both.

I don't think Goliath had any apprehension. He was super confident that his size, strength, armor and overwhelming weaponry were no match for this kid. He would crush the boy and feed him to the vultures. The Philistine army would impose their will on the obstinate Israelites and make them pay for the insult of not properly responding to their champion's challenge.

Now we know the thinking of David's opponent:

- He clearly hates God.
- He is utterly confident in his own strength and ability.

- He supports his own (false) gods. Whether he really believes in them and worships them is another matter.

What Goliath does not realize, never even considers, is that he is a puppet. He and the whole Philistine army are agents of Satan, only they do not know it. Goliath is the mouthpiece for the real and mortal enemy. Satan intends to crush David and thwart God's plans for Israel.

For Reflection

Think about the battle you are facing. Are you ready to take the risk involved? What are the stakes? Are you committed to fight until the end?

2

David Responds

Then David said to the Philistine, "You come to me with a sword and with a spear and with a javelin, but I come to you in the name of the LORD of hosts."

1 Samuel 17:45

David proclaims the truth and does not care who hears him. He is not concerned with political correctness.

First, he states the obvious: "You come to me with a sword and with a spear and with a javelin." David acknowledges the superior weaponry of the Philistine. "But I . . ." David does not bother declaring his weapons. Rather he proclaims his authority in this confrontation. "I come to you in the name of the LORD of hosts, the God of the armies of Israel, whom you have defied. This day the LORD will deliver you into my hand" (verses 45–46).

David is both a soldier and a prophet. Under the power of the Holy Spirit, he proclaims that Israel's God is the one real God. David never considers negotiation—there is nothing to negotiate with the enemy who defies God. David is not interested in an ecumenical movement. That was a large part of Israel's problem—they thought pagan cultures and foreign religions could coexist in a nation under one God.

There is something powerful when a situation is so clearly black and white. In this day, we have developed an appetite for compromise, for tolerance, for ecumenism. All points of view are valid. This syncretism plays more of a role in our churches than we realize. Without consciously thinking about it, many Christians accept that all roads lead to God.

Jesus says, "I am the way." Modern "experts" say, "That can't be right. That's your truth but not my truth. You can't impose your truth on me."

Well, David is about to impose the truth on Goliath. He starts by declaring the truth.

David is terribly bold. Why are we so timid? Because people will accuse us of being intolerant? Are we afraid of the possible consequences? David does not care. He must state what to him is obvious. This may seem risky. What if . . . ? What if God does not come through? What if David loses this fight?

No, David knows exactly what he is doing. Any Israelite could have done the same. Each Hebrew had the right to live in utter dependence on God. Regrettably, they did not trust Him like David did. They did not really know God. If they had spent less time cowering in fear and more time in Scripture, they would have understood the faithfulness God had shown to Abraham and Joseph and Moses. They should have spent the hours between Goliath's morning and evening insults immersed in the book of Joshua to see how God fought for the Hebrews and drove the pagans out of the land.

I am impressed today with how some brethren in the Persecuted Church understand this truth. For them, there is no dialogue or cooperation with their oppressors. Their choice is simple: proclamation of the Gospel, then imprisonment. As you can see, that is really no choice! The Church in Russia and China has gone through great tribulation. In the process, they settled this issue. They simply would not keep silent about Jesus. Whereas we in the free world, well, too many hardly acknowledge they know Him.

The Persecuted Church shows us how to live by faith in the midst of spiritual war. That is why I believe the Persecuted Church is the Church of the future. In fact, it may be the only genuine Church in the world today.[1]

David knew the truth. David declared the truth. Then David acted on the truth. That is why David could confidently announce the outcome of this confrontation.

For Reflection

How do you know and act on the truth? What authority does this give you as you confront your giant?

3

The Reason for the Battle

This day the LORD will deliver you into my hand, and I will strike you down and cut off your head.

1 Samuel 17:46

Did David really understand the situation? I mean, he was too young to know systematic theology and doctrines of spiritual conflict. Clearly he was not quoting Scripture when he shouted to the Philistine.

Remember that David is under the influence of the Holy Spirit. When you are Spirit controlled and proclaim the Word of God under His authority and power, there is a lot of liberty to say what you want. I am not suggesting you make things up. I am saying that the Gospel should be such a part of our lives that when we speak, we speak the truth of the Gospel, however we may articulate it.

Paul the apostle says, "If you confess with your mouth that Jesus is Lord [declaration, proclamation] and believe in your heart that God raised him from the dead, you will be saved" (Romans 10:9). We must never water down the Gospel. David believed with his whole heart what God revealed in Scripture. He declared what he knew. Then he expected God to save him or to kill the giant.

This is not how most humans do battle today. On a human level, when two countries are at war, their diplomats behind the scenes seek a solution. Often there is some give and take. This situation in Elah Valley was very different because David versus Goliath was ultimately a spiritual battle.

Here we have the forces of hell against God. You do not strike deals with the enemies of God. God's honor is at stake.

We are in a mess today because we compromise with the enemy rather than trust God and what He has promised. Too many people are Christians on Sunday (or just a couple of hours on Sunday), but God has little or no part in their lives the rest of the week.

David seems to get a little carried away in his declaration. He promises to strike down Goliath and cut off his head. Then "I will give the dead bodies of the host of the Philistines this day to the birds of the air and to the wild beasts of the earth" (verse 46). Whoa, wait a minute! The deal was that the army of the loser serve the army of the victor. No one said anything about one army slaughtering the other. David has exceeded his authority. He has just committed Israel to war.

That is correct because David knew the nation's rights. These pagans had no right being in Israel. Their gods could never coexist with Israel's God. Compromise was not an option—only total victory by God and for God and His people. The Philistines should have been annihilated two hundred or more years earlier. They were not. So David has started a fight of which God approves.

By now it should be clear that David is not fighting for a reward. We never even hear that he claimed the prize for his victory. Those rewards were infinitely small compared to the single big issue.

David is fighting with the right motive. He wants to bear witness. Listen: "That all the earth may know that there is a God in Israel" (verse 46). Come on, David. Is that not hyperbole? No. The whole earth *does* know. The story has been told and retold in picture books and storybooks and movies. David continues. "That all this assembly may know that the LORD saves not with sword and spear" (verse 47). Well, Israel has no spear and only two swords. This battle is designed for the people of God to witness the power of their God. Finally, "For the battle is the LORD's, and he will give you into our hand."

So, there it is. Let the fight begin!

For Reflection

What is the evidence that you/we are engaged in spiritual battle? What witness do you bring to this battle?

4

To the Death

David ran quickly toward the battle line to meet the Philistine.

1 Samuel 17:48

Goliath was angry. The kid really intended to fight him. He got up and lumbered toward David. He couldn't move very quickly. He was huge, bulky and was carrying a couple hundred pounds of equipment.

David was limber, quick. He *ran* to the battle.

If this story were novelized, it would be a very short book. This is not a made-for-television special. If it were, there would be far more drama—ninety minutes, at least, with commercials.

Many years ago, Al recalls seeing a movie of the Bible that included this battle. David dodged and feinted. Goliath swung his sword and missed. David shot a stone, and it clanged off the giant's armor. Goliath took another swipe, and David skipped out of harm's way. How long did the scene last? I can assure you that the movie version took a lot longer than the actual battle.

David ran toward the giant. No trickery here.

David reached into his shepherd's bag and pulled out a stone. Deftly, he loaded his sling. As he got closer, he whirled the sling furiously. Goliath never got a chance to use his superior strength because David let fly with the stone. It was a perfect shot smack in the middle of the giant's forehead. The stone found a welcome and empty skull!

Goliath did not know what hit him. Like a giant tree, he slowly starts to fall, picks up speed and lands face first on the ground.

David does not have a moment to waste. There is no time for a celebration because the giant is not dead—not yet.

David promised to cut off the Philistine's head. He has no sword, but the giant does. It is still in its sheath. David pulls out the sword and delivers the mortal thrust into the neck. Then he finishes the job, sawing the head from the body.

Still no time to celebrate. There remained an army to destroy. By removing the head of Goliath, David had also chopped off the head of the Philistine military. Like a headless body, the Philistine forces go into convulsions. Trained soldiers panic and flee. Some drop their weapons—Israel re-armed that day. As the Israelite army pursues the enemy, it is a slaughter. Bodies are strewn from Socoh to the gates of Ekron and Gath, the main Philistine cities. Then the Hebrew soldiers take their time stripping the armor and swords off their fallen enemies. Next time there is an attack on the nation, they would be equipped and ready.

There is one interesting observation we should make. It appears that something important is missing from this story. There is no prayer service before the battle. Saul does not call a prayer meeting. David does not request of his friends: "Pray for me." Given the significance of this event, we might expect to see that detail recorded. Isn't that curious? Not really. Prayer is not the habit of a backslidden nation. Maybe that was the first activity they dropped. No wonder they were so afraid.

I think another reason prayer is not mentioned is because David obeys God and runs to the challenge, trusting in God. The pious may insist we pray first. Fine. Pray! David is a man of prayer—read the psalms; he wrote half of them. But here David realizes that it is time to *act*, to *fight*. This is not the time for a prayer meeting. It is a time for action.

Never substitute prayer for obedience!

I believe in prayer, of course. It has always been central to our work and ministry. But when God sends you on a mission, *go!*

I need to add that David was prepared to go. There was no deceit in him—that was his secret. Too many Christians lead double lives—pious on the outside, rotten on the inside. If that describes you, then you will fail when you confront your giant. David succeeded because he lived a life of devotion to God. It was daily. His communion with God was often in solitude. When God called him to take action, he was ready.

You know the results. Now you also know the reason for those results.

--- **For Reflection** ---

What lessons do you take away from David's battle with Goliath that apply to your life and the spiritual battles you face?

5

The War Isn't Over Yet

Then [David] . . . chose five smooth stones from the brook and put them in his shepherd's pouch.

1 Samuel 17:40

Why did David pick five stones when he needed only one? I believe David was making a prophetic statement. Goliath had four brothers. When David killed Goliath, his brothers would want revenge. David was ready for them.

It is important to remember that winning one battle rarely means that the war is over. Someone has said that eternal vigilance is the price of liberty. We must maintain vigilance as

Christians because the spiritual world war will continue until Jesus destroys every rule and authority and power on earth.

It is worth noting that God did not call David to fight all the giants. Just one! Once David had demonstrated that giants could be brought down, God allowed others to join the fun. Those heroics are recorded in 2 Samuel 21. The brutal fact is that these giants had to be annihilated, otherwise they would continue to pose a threat to the first coming of Jesus.

We should also note that Israel did not really finish the job. Once the giant was dead, Israel drove the Philistines off their land and back to their own cities. Good! The enemy was back where they belonged. They should have been driven out of the land long ago. Then Saul's army backs off and they plunder the Philistine camp. Well, that is good, too. They finally arm themselves with proper weapons.

I wonder, though, if they should have stayed more focused on their counterattack. Before long, the Philistines were able to regroup, and they continued to plague Israel for many more years. What if Israel had decided enough is enough, laid siege to Gath and Ekron and the other Philistine cities, and determined that these pagans would never again be a threat to God's people?

Today the devil continues to try to frustrate the plans of God. He failed to prevent the incarnation. His head was bruised at Calvary (fulfilling Genesis 3:15). Now he seeks revenge against the Church, against the people of God. He is doing all he can to thwart the advance of God's Kingdom.

God uses David as a type of Jesus, the Great Shepherd who defeats the real enemy of us all. In Goliath, the uncircumcised Philistine, we see one type of unbelief. Let's use today's label: atheism. In recent years, several books by clever scientists have sought to convince us that there is no God. He is a myth, a figment of our imaginations. We are products of chance and evolution. These "experts" make loud and powerful arguments and gain considerable attention in the media. Sounds like Goliath all over again.

How do we fight the giant of atheism? Our best weapon is faith. It does not need to be mature faith. David was just a boy. Despite having little experience in the world, his faith was enough to defeat the atheistic giant. Even at age fifteen or sixteen he was not about to let the uncircumcised Philistine trample the armies of God. Here the teenager was far ahead of the adults in Israel. He saw his countrymen as the army of the living God; however, the army also needed to believe this if they were to be effective.

What did the people of Israel gain from David's victory? For sure that day they regained some dignity. They were no longer the helpless, fearful, intimidated farmers who could not even forge a few swords to defend themselves. They enjoyed a great victory. Except it was artificial. It was like a football player scoring a great goal and all the fans declaring, "*We* did it. *We* won!"

The fact is Israel did not do anything to deserve or achieve this win. God did it all through one faithful servant; however, the people could have used this as a chance to learn more about God. They could have returned home to serve heartily the God who promised to protect them if they followed Him and who would abandon them if they did not.

Did the people truly understand the significance of this victory? When Israel's soldiers returned to their homes and lay down in their beds, did the trauma of those forty days still haunt them? I wonder if the echoes of the giant's voice reverberated in their minds. Such brainwashing leaves deep scars.

Remember: *Do not fear!* If God is with you, there is no reason to be afraid.

Sure, it is dangerous to take on a giant like atheism. It is dangerous to stand up in public for the honor of God, whatever the issue. You will become a target. Enemies will shoot at you. Friends may abandon you. That is the risk we take. That is the war we must fight today.

For Reflection

How do you react to fearful news in your country? It might concern the influx of immigrants or the push to redefine marriage. Perhaps it is the latest health scare or economic crisis. How does the example of David provide you with insights into how you might respond?

Am I Ready to Fight?

For the weapons of our warfare are not of the flesh but have divine power to destroy strongholds.

2 Corinthians 10:4

Are you ready to confront the giant God allows in your life? Perhaps you cannot know for sure until you confront him. Still there are some indications when you are ready. You see, the real battle with Goliath took place in David's heart. He learned to know God in the private place where no one could see him—as he took care of the sheep. He listened to the Spirit God placed in him when he was anointed; therefore, he was able to discern the situation as he arrived at the battlefield.

There are three ways we can prove we are fighting the battles God has chosen for us.

First, we prove it by our motive. We do not seek anything for ourselves. We aim solely for God's glory. There is a famous saying that says, "There is no limit to what we can accomplish when we don't care who gets the credit." I would amend that. There is no limit to what we can accomplish when our aim is to make sure *God* gets *all* the credit. If my motive is God's glory and I do not care about my life, then I can dare to do anything. Jesus said, "Whoever finds his life will lose it, and whoever loses his life for my sake will find it" (Matthew 10:39).

Second, we prove it by our method. We dare not fire the Lord's cannons with the devil's powder. The apostle Paul says that we do not wage war the way the world does. Our weapons of warfare are not human but divine. We have the resources of Scripture, the Holy Spirit and the collective power of the Church of Jesus Christ to destroy arguments and every lofty opinion raised against the knowledge of God (see 2 Corinthians 10:4–5). We prepare for battle by taking every thought we have captive to obey Christ. Like David, our weapons are testimony and proclamation.

So much of prophecy and teaching today focuses on "my life, my health, my future, my happiness." The devil likes that because his focus is to destroy God's Kingdom, and our self-centeredness is one of his best weapons. He knows ultimately Jesus will win but he wants Jesus to offer a pitiful gift to His Father—just a few souls, not a great harvest. Let's wake up to the devil's strategy! Let's not allow him to keep diverting us from the heart of Jesus. Go and make disciples of all peoples. If each one of us does his or her part, Jesus will present to the Father a powerful and glorious Kingdom.

Finally, we prove a battle is the right one by our faith. This is a faith that compels us to proclaim the truth. One of my favorite examples is that of Corrie ten Boom when she was speaking in what was then East Germany. She was scheduled to speak in a cathedral, and it was packed with thousands, with more gathered outside wanting to hear her. This was a Communist country. Preaching was confined to the church building.

Not for Corrie! She went to see the mayor and said, "I need loudspeakers so the crowd outside the cathedral can hear." You can imagine the mayor's reaction. Corrie didn't back down. "You know that Jesus is the victor, don't you?" she asked, no doubt reminding the man of his Christian roots as a boy.

"Uh, yes. I guess."

"Then you know what to do!"

Within an hour there were loudspeakers outside the cathedral and half the city heard her preach.[1]

That is boldness that emerges from faith, knowing your cause is right. You determine: "I'm going to proclaim the truth and fight." This was David's example: words followed by action.

Today there is too much talk without action. Let's change that. Let's step up and demonstrate our faith to a world that needs to see how powerful our God really is.

We have a tremendous task ahead of us. May God help us gain insight into the giants we must confront. May He give us the skill to proclaim the truth about Him and then the faith to act and see the battle through to its conclusion.

Are you ready? Then go in the power of the Spirit!

For Reflection

Whether you are facing a giant right now or will face one in the future, are you prepared? Take a few moments to reflect on your motives, your methods and your faith.

The Carmel Judgment

Then Elijah said to the prophets of Baal, "Choose for your-selves one bull and prepare it first, for you are many, and call upon the name of your god, but put no fire to it."

1 Kings 18:25

Then Elijah said to all the people, "Come near to me."

1 Kings 18:30

Elijah represents God's side in this contest against Baal. Elijah is also the referee.

Observers might protest that this contest is rigged. Well, it is! God establishes the rules. He also plays by His rules.

179

This is not *mano a mano* but *Deo a deo*. Elijah is *not* a player. He simply prepares the playing field for the divine contest.

Elijah spells out the rules. There will be two bulls cut into pieces and laid on a pile of wood atop an altar. No one will light a match. Each side will call on its god and the one who answers with fire wins.

There are two halves to this event. Elijah defers to the prophets of Baal—the first half belongs to them. They prepare the bull, place it on a pile of wood and begin to pray. From morning until noon, they plead for Baal to answer them and ignite the pyre.

It was the custom of this deity's priests to gash themselves, hoping somehow this might rouse their god. There is no historical record that Baal ever performed a single miracle. What did these men expect? Why such confidence in Baal?

Elijah's response was to mock them. Elijah notes that Baal could be traveling or asleep. Or, perhaps, he has gone to the bathroom! Give him a moment to clean up and he will come to you! This only provoked the prophets to increase the intensity of their rituals. Four hundred and fifty voices can make a lot of noise. Four hundred and fifty priests of Baal cutting themselves spills a lot of blood. Surely that ought to get the attention of any proper deity!

Elijah is not impressed. Is mockery a legitimate part of prophetic ministry? It does not seem very loving or tolerant. Surely Elijah could be just a little kinder. Or keep quiet and let the drama play out.

There is a time when the truth must be proclaimed. True love requires it. Unless we begin to call the enemy by his proper name, others will never identify the real adversary of our souls.

The first half of the contest concludes. There is no score.

Elijah begins the second half with these instructions to the people: "Come near to me." He cannot wait to show off what God is about to do. Plus, everyone will see there is absolutely no trickery involved. No magician could make this up. So gather round. Observe carefully!

God's Spirit directs Elijah every step of the way. The first job is to rebuild the altar of God. Elijah then digs a trench around the altar. He places wood—Mount Carmel had many trees, and due to the drought, there were plenty of dry branches available. Then he slices the throat of the bull, cuts the animal in pieces and lays it on the wood.

Elijah has one more order of business before God shows up. Water!

Four jars are filled with water and poured over the offering on the altar, soaking the animal and the wood. How did the people respond to that? With a little laughter? Crazy Elijah!

Elijah is not finished. Do it a second time. Four more jars of water are poured over Yahweh's altar. Do it again! Now the water has run down and filled the trench. There is no way that any spark can accidently ignite this offering.

Now, come closer—but not too close—you do not want to get scorched. Can you feel the tension?

The sad thing is that the people could have avoided this ecological crisis. God had warned them centuries before that if they worshiped Him, He would provide rain and bless their crops. It was all recorded in written form. They just had to read Scripture (see Deuteronomy 11:16–17). Their Bibles, however, were hidden and gathering dust.

How will people know the truth if they do not read the Bible? Well, this crowd is not reading the Scripture passages delivered to them by Moses. They are ignoring the prophets, or worse, persecuting them. Even killing them. Elijah must plug the gap. For now, he is their Bible.

Let's not tell unbelievers to read the Bible. You are the Bible! If they cannot read you, they will not read the other book. That is the situation here: Elijah at this moment is the Word from God.

The crowd holds its breath.

Elijah prays.

For Reflection

Have you ever been in a situation where you were doomed to failure unless God showed up? What happened?

Victory!

"Answer me, O LORD, answer me, that this people may know that you, O LORD, are God, and that you have turned their hearts back." Then the fire of the LORD fell and consumed the burnt offering and the wood and the stones and the dust, and licked up the water that was in the trench.

1 Kings 18:37–38

Elijah prays very specifically to the "Lord God of Abraham, Isaac and Israel"—the patriarchs. This reflects the revelation made to Moses at the burning bush—this is the God who has guided Abraham's descendants for centuries. Elijah prays that this God—*Yahweh*, I AM—will reveal Himself as God in Israel,

183

and that "I am your servant, and that I have done all these things at your word" (verse 36)

Remember this was not Elijah's idea. God scheduled this Super Bowl, this World Cup, this Olympic showdown to conclusively demonstrate to a rebel nation who is really in charge.

Everyone holds their breath. What a huge risk the prophet is taking. Yet Elijah has lived all his life for this very moment. It could have been a real crisis, except Elijah was prepared. Crisis management does not work for Christians. Our response in crisis is the outcome of our daily walk. If you have not learned to live with Jesus, to live in the Word and to see miracles as your prayers are answered, then you probably will not want to take a huge risk. You will not handle crisis well.

We need the patience, the discipline and the persistence of walking with God. Without years of training in secret, Elijah could not have handled the tension of this contest. Elijah was confident in the God who had provided for him at Cherith brook and in the widow's home in Zarephath. He had faced the impossible situation of the widow's dead son and had witnessed the miracle of God bringing the boy back to life. So Elijah was ready.

How long did everyone wait for the fire? Not long. God was ready to act the moment Elijah prayed. That is important—because God wanted the crowd to know that He heard this prayer, and this was His answer.

What a spectacle He put on. Better than any fireworks show. In fact, you might think He overdid it a little. Fire came down from heaven and burned up the bull and the wood. It burned up the stones of the altar and the dust around the altar. The fire even "licked up the water that was in the trench" (verse 38).

It must have been stunning. No one in this crowd had seen such a miracle. Well, except Elijah.

I imagine there was a moment of stunned silence. Then like a crowd at a major sports event, the viewers erupted in a roar. They began to cheer.

"The Lord, He is God!"

"The Lord, He is God!"

What did that sound like? It sounded like this: "Elijah! Elijah!"

Remember, this is what Elijah's name means: Yahweh is my God.

Elijah. The Lord, He is God.

How would the prophet respond to that?

This is Elijah's great moment. Surely this marks a turning point in Israel's history. Just listen to their roar and chants; however, what has really changed? Have the people truly repented? Is their ecstasy a signal that they have finally seen the light? Or are they simply admiring the show and cheering for the hero of the day?

Why did the people not immediately fall down, confess their sin and commit to worship the one true God? The word from the prophet should have been enough for the people. Why do we have to wait for signs and wonders?

Why do we seek the spectacular? The Word of God should be sufficient.

A sad fact: If the Word is not sufficient, neither are supernatural wonders. That is the problem with miracles—their impact rarely seems to last. Elijah challenged the crowd to choose. Instead, they waited to see which deity would win. Those miracles in Exodus were so six hundred years ago. They wanted their own show.

Now God had conclusively proved His claim to be Israel's one true God. Israel was pointed back to the covenant, made with Abraham, renewed under Moses. With such a decisive outcome to the battle of altars, would the people destroy the idols, tear down Baal's temple, burn the Asherah poles on the high places? Would they stand against the terrorism of the prophets by Ahab's wife?

For Reflection

What convinces you that the Lord is God?

3

Run for Your Life!

Ahab told Jezebel all that Elijah had done, and how he had killed all the prophets with the sword. Then Jezebel sent a messenger to Elijah saying, "So may the gods do to me and more also, if I do not make your life as the life of one of them by this time tomorrow."

1 Kings 19:1–2

After the triumph on Mount Carmel, Elijah ordered the arrest and execution of the 450 false prophets of Baal. Then he dismissed the crowd and begged God to send rain. Finally, the sky grew dark and Elijah, still energized by the Spirit and adrenaline, started running. He sprinted twenty miles to

Jezreel and arrived before King Ahab's chariot. This is when the great warrior/prophet began to falter.

When we have engaged in battle, especially one as intense as the confrontation on Mount Carmel, we need a break. Unfortunately, the enemy refuses to cooperate. He looks for weakness, for a vulnerability he can attack. In this case, Elijah's kryptonite is Ahab's wife. As soon as the king arrives in Jezreel, he rushes into his castle to report on the day's events. Ahab had to tell Jezebel how her god was soundly defeated. Interesting that Ahab did not order her to attend. Probably because she would have disrupted things.

The more Jezebel hears, the angrier she gets. Her plans for the Baalization of Israel have suffered a huge setback. She could, of course, surrender. What more evidence does she need that Yahweh is Israel's true and only God? But whether she knows it or not, Jezebel is under enemy control. The devil recognizes a willing hostess when he sees one. This woman will never repent. She will never compromise. Under Satan's inspiration she is determined to get revenge.

Jezebel's scream is heard throughout the palace. "I have a message for Elijah," she yells. A servant rushes to her office to take dictation. "May the gods do to me and more also, if I do not make your life as the life of one of them (the Baal prophets) by this time tomorrow. That's the message. Now go!" (see verse 2).

The messenger did not have to go far to find God's prophet— he was hanging around the gates of Jezreel. What Elijah hears is, "In twenty-four hours, you're a dead man." This is no idle threat. Jezebel has delivered in the past.

But Elijah has survived worse. He has seen God protect him and demonstrate His superiority at every point. There is no reason to panic.

What happened to our bold, radical, courageous prophet? The one who listened for God's instructions and obeyed? Who fearlessly challenged 450 prophets of the dominant culture? Who interceded for the people until desperately needed rain arrived? It is as though Elijah loses his mind. I think it began when he raced Ahab to Jezreel. The Spirit of the Lord was on Elijah, but did the Spirit tell him to undertake this superhuman feat?

Elijah flees, heading south to Beersheba. That is about 120 miles. How long did it take him? We don't know. Did he run, or procure a horse? Apart from his servant, he was all alone. He had no friend to slow him down, pray with him, encourage him. He would have passed by Jerusalem, but he paid no visit to the Temple.

Elijah's servant finally quits. The prophet leaves him in Beersheba and continues into the wilderness. Finally, beyond the reach of his vicious enemy, he lies down and goes to sleep. But first listen to his pitiful prayer: "It is enough; now, O LORD, take away my life, for I am no better than my fathers" (1 Kings 19:4).

There is a serious warning here. Spiritual battles are exhausting. While we may be called to superhuman assignments, we are not superheroes with unlimited human abilities. We can burn out. We can be depleted physically, emotionally, spiritually. We can suffer from PTSD—post traumatic stress disorder. We may experience depression. We likely will lose our desire and ability to practice spiritual disciplines. That is when we need others in the Body of Christ to come alongside us.

But Elijah had no one. So God sent an angel.

Notice God's gracious provision. The angel touches Elijah and tells him to wake up and eat. A lovely meal is provided, a freshly baked cake and a jar of water. Elijah accepts the food, then goes back to sleep. After a good night's rest, Elijah is awakened again by the angel and told to get up and eat, "for the journey is too great for you" (verse 7). Thus fortified, Elijah travels for the next forty days and nights to Mount Horeb, the mountain of God, also known as Mount Sinai. Here, Elijah will have his most personal encounter with God.

For Reflection

What is your plan to protect your health—emotional as well as physical—in the midst of intense ministry? Consider things like daily time with God, gathering with other believers and occasional retreats where you get away to be renewed.

4

Journey into a Cave

He arose and ate and drank, and went in the strength of that food forty days and forty nights to Horeb, the mount of God. There he came to a cave and lodged in it.

1 Kings 19:8–9

Elijah had a long, lonely journey to Mount Sinai. It had to be a challenge hiking over that dry and rugged terrain.

Let's imagine what the prophet was thinking as he trudged through the wilderness. No doubt he relived the key moments of his life and ministry. He recalled his first encounter with King Ahab where he announced that the clouds had dried up. Then a year or more alone at Cherith brook, and two more years living with the foreign widow and her son. Those were lonely years—just him and God. No fellow prophets to talk with and discuss the trials of ministry.

Finally came the call to action. Elijah relived the drama on Mount Carmel. For a brief moment, all the political and religious leaders and influencers were riveted by the contest. No doubt, Elijah won a great victory. The story would be told and retold by all who witnessed that drama.

But he had blood on his hands—450 prophets of Baal executed by his order. He still saw their lifeless bodies falling into the Kishon brook. One does not easily erase such memories.

As the crowd headed home, he was all alone again, praying for mercy on a rebellious, unworthy nation. The land was so dry. *Lord, please bring rain.* The point had been made—the one and only Yahweh, not Baal, controlled the weather. Where were those clouds? Seven times he had his servant go look over the sea. Finally, God answered Elijah's prayer, but the work of intercession left him fatigued.

Then the threats from the evil queen came—how much could one man endure? At least now Jezebel could not reach him. If she even knew where he was, she had to figure he was as good as dead in this God and Baal-forsaken terrain.

Among all those swirling memories replaying in his mind, one thought took root and came to dominate his thoughts. It was a speech. If God gave him a chance, he was going to recite a few facts of life. He would tell His Master in the strongest voice possible: *I have been very jealous for the Lord, the God of hosts. For the people of Israel have forsaken Your covenant, thrown down Your altars and killed Your prophets with the sword, and I, even I only, am left, and they seek my life to take it away.*

Yes, he would give God a piece of his mind. Look how much he had given up to serve Yahweh. He had obeyed every divine command. So, where was the revival? Why had the people not stood up and protested Ahab and his wicked wife? What did he have to show for all of his sermons and the great demonstration on Carmel? Nothing! This just was not fair.

Finally, Elijah saw the mountain in the distance. A surge of energy helped him pick up the pace. What would he find on Sinai? Would he meet God as Moses had centuries before? Maybe here he would get answers.

Elijah reached the base of the mountain and began to carefully climb the rocky terrain. There were no trees and few shrubs. The summit looked blackened—maybe that was remnant of an earlier time when God met the Israelites with fire and lightening and smoke (see Exodus 19) after they escaped Pharaoh's bondage.

Elijah did not want to spend the night on the slope exposed to the elements. He saw a cave a couple of hundred feet above him. Carefully clamoring over some boulders, he entered the cool shade. Here, he could rest. He retreated into the darkness. He wrapped his cloak around him and sat down. His eyes drooped. He was tired. Forty long days walking. He needed to sleep.

Only he could not. A familiar voice interrupted: "Elijah, what are you doing here?"

For Reflection

Have you ever experienced depression like Elijah? Were you, or are you, so tired, so emotionally spent that you feel you cannot go any further? What would you like to say to God about how you feel? Be honest!

5

Hush. Pay Attention!

And he said, "Go and stand on the mount before the LORD."
And behold, the LORD passed by.

1 Kings 19:11

Have you ever been in a cave? At night? Alone, because you are out of touch with God? It is a depressing situation.

Elijah sat in a cave on Mount Sinai. We do not know how long. Scripture just tells us Elijah came to a cave and the Word of God came to him. It started with a question.

Our prophet answered with his litany of complaints. "I have been very jealous for the LORD" (verse 14). It is good that someone feels so passionate for God's reputation. But

Elijah had assumed a greater burden than God required. God's servant was looking at the huge population of Israel. He focused on their rebellion against God. He saw all their wicked behaviors and internalized it. It left him stressed, burned out and spent.

So God removed him from the field. Elijah no longer saw the forbidden idols. He was out of touch with the royal palace. There was no entertainment to distract him. Elijah was alone with his thoughts. Until God showed up.

In solitude, Elijah prepared for a transformational moment. He received these instructions: Go and stand before the Lord. What does this mean? It means that Elijah is going to get perspective. Not necessarily answers. God is not required to answer questions such as, Why, Lord, do You permit evil in this world? God rarely answers our why questions. Instead, He reveals something far more important. Let's observe what happens.

God tells Elijah to stand before the Lord. Then "behold, the LORD passed by" (verse 11). This reminds us of Moses' encounter with God on the same mountain. Moses had asked God to show him His glory. God had hidden Moses in a cleft of a rock while His glory passed by, then allowed Israel's rescuer to see His back. As God passed before Moses, He proclaimed that He is merciful and gracious, slow to anger and abounding in love (see Exodus 34:5–8). This was a transformational moment for Moses and the nation. In the centuries that followed, every prophet harkened back to that revelation.

Perhaps Elijah expected to see that glory or to hear those same comforting words. That was not going to happen. No two encounters with God are identical. Elijah and Moses met Yahweh on the same mountain. But the revelations were unique. Elijah received a demonstration of nature's power. First a "great and strong wind" with tornado force tore rocks on the mountain to pieces. Elijah retreated into his cave to escape the flying debris that might cut him or knock him out. Such raw power he had never seen before.

But the Lord was not in the wind.

Then the earth began to shake. The cave could not protect him as he heard the rumble and felt the mountain vibrate around him. Dirt and dust poured over him as the earth quaked for one, two—how long?—very long minutes. God was putting on a show for His servant.

But the Lord was not in the earthquake.

The stillness that followed was a relief. There were no aftershocks. Elijah waited. Next he saw the light, and the cave, until then a cool sixty degrees, began to heat up alarmingly. He retreated as far back as possible to escape the flames licking at the cave's entrance. Was this God's holy, burning flame that led Israel in the wilderness?

No, the Lord was not in the fire.

The flames retreated. The temperature started to drop. The silence was deafening. The prophet waited. Then there was a faint sound. Yet clear, distinct. Just a whisper.

Elijah moved back to the entrance of the cave. Unlike the raw power of nature, this quiet voice terrified him. He pulled up his cloak over his face.

Finally, God had a conversation with His emotionally distraught servant.

For Reflection

We all need to gain perspective, but that is hard to obtain from the internet, cable news or the many opinions of people around us. We need times of solitude and silence so that God can speak to us. Where do you go to be alone with God? How do you recognize His voice when He speaks?

6

Your Next Assignment

The Lord said to him, "Go, return on your way to the wilderness of Damascus . . . and Elisha the son of Shaphat of Abel-meholah you shall anoint to be prophet in your place."

1 Kings 19:15–16

"What are you doing here?"

God's annoying question yet again. How many times had Elijah recited the speech in his mind? "I have been very jealous. . . . I, even I only am left. . . ."

Will God provide an answer? First, the Lord has instructions for Elijah: "Go back the way you came. In Damascus, anoint Hazael to be king over Syria. Then go and anoint Jehu

199

to be King of Israel." Yes, Ahab's days are numbered! Good news: God has a replacement for the evil king and queen.

Then, Elijah, anoint your successor. Elisha will take your place as Israel's prophet. The judgment of God will continue through these three men. If anyone escapes the word of Hazael, Jehu will be executioner. Those who escape the word of Jehu will have to face Elisha.

Now, Elijah, listen carefully: "I'm preserving for myself seven thousand souls; the knees that haven't bowed to the god Baal, the mouths that haven't kissed his image" (1 Kings 19:18 MSG).

Elijah had no idea. He knew Obadiah, Ahab's trusted servant, had hidden and fed one hundred prophets. But there were others? Seven thousand!

What did Elijah think when he received that information? Maybe, *Where were they when I stood all alone on Mount Carmel?*

What were these seven thousand people doing? Could any of these men and women be enlisted in the spiritual war raging in Israel? They had to be disturbed by the moral decline of their country. Could any of them have come alongside Elijah, put an arm around him, prayed with him, stood with him against the horde of Baal's prophets?

Could they have joined Elijah in the fight? Maybe some tried, only to quickly encounter opposition. They were lonely voices in a cacophony of Baal's voices broadcasting another message. If they tried to convert any of the pagans around them, Jezebel would hear about it, and she was ruthless.

Imagine that you are a soldier. Your commanding officer has ordered you to invade enemy-held territory. But as you move forward, you discover the enemy's defenses are formidable. You hear the roar of guns, and there are explosions all around you. So you report back to headquarters, and your commanding officer asks, "Well, did you capture that position?"

"No, sir," you reply. "The enemy won't let me."

Do you think you can get away with that answer? Is that not what warfare is all about? When a soldier receives an order, he is bound by his oath of allegiance to fight to the death to fulfill it. He will not let himself be stopped simply because the enemy is entrenched and armed and resistant. The obstruction must be overcome if the battle is to be won.

Exactly the same principle of allegiance and obedience applies to spiritual warfare where we may have to disobey civil authorities in order to obey the Lord's command. Yet a lot of Christian soldiers seem to be saying to their Commander, "We can't advance because the enemy disapproves of our objectives."

Of course the devil does not approve! That is what makes him the enemy. Why are so many Christians amazed and immobilized by the least sign of resistance to the Gospel? I believe it is because we have forgotten who issued our orders.

Seven thousand potential warriors could have made a huge difference in Israel. But they were hidden and ineffective. Society was going to hell, and they said nothing, did nothing. No wonder Elijah fell into depression.

The fundamental principle for all Christian work is this: The Lord Jesus Christ, who crushed Satan and conquered death, commands us to invade this enemy-occupied world and reclaim it for God. We march under His authority.

This battle was not Elijah's alone to fight. Others could have signed up to serve with him.

Still, Elijah heard good news. There was hope. He would find Elisha and mentor him, prepare him for ministry. Maybe together they could search out those hidden believers who had not submitted to Baal. They could start a Bible school and train them in Scripture. These recruits could then join them in the battle for the soul of a nation.

For Reflection

Have you received an assignment from God? What opposition do you face? God has something for you to do that will advance His Kingdom despite opposition.

1

A Long Walk in the Right Direction

Go to Nineveh, that great city, and call out against it the message that I tell you.

Jonah 3:2

Jonah arose and went to Nineveh, according to the word of the LORD.

Jonah 3:3

Jonah goes to Nineveh not to entertain but to proclaim. His preaching is the solution to the terrorism of the Assyrians.

Jonah probably walked to Nineveh. It is approximately four hundred miles from the Mediterranean Sea to Assyria's capital city just east of the Tigris River. If he walked twenty miles a day, that is twenty long days. No one offered him a ride—one look at him and travelers moved quickly away.

How did Jonah use the time? He could have planned some messages, but since God had told him what to say, there were no messages to write. So he probably did a lot of thinking. Naturally, Jonah was grateful to be alive. Still, he was going where he did not want to go. To Assyria. To his enemies. He could not help but think of what they had done to his people. Worse, he was traveling there without the permission of King Jeroboam. This would be considered treason, unless . . .

The northern kingdom of Israel had struggled to solve the problem of the Assyrians. They had debated various solutions. Should they attempt to work through diplomatic channels— registering protests in the courts of all the neighboring counties? Or should they launch an economic boycott? It would certainly hurt the Assyrians if the trade routes through Israel and Judah were blocked. Or should they attempt to destroy them militarily? King Jeroboam II had experienced some military success. But could his forces stand against the most powerful military in the world? Would the people support him if the campaign lasted several years? How many Israelite children would die before the people demanded that their husbands and sons return?

None of these options seemed attractive. Jonah knew. He had heard all of them argued by the king's advisers. Now Jonah was going to Nineveh, but he was not carrying diplomatic papers from the king. Jonah's orders came from a higher authority. Go and preach!

Since when did preaching ever solve the problem of terrorism? Jonah had heard the hawks say over and over, "The only thing those Assyrians understand is force."

God had told Jonah to go to Nineveh and preach against it. Jonah ran away, and look at all the problems that caused him. Now Jonah obeyed. This time God's instructions were more specific: "Go and proclaim the message I give you."

The message was precise: "In forty days, Nineveh will be destroyed!" This improved Jonah's outlook. How would God do it? It needed to be something horrific—to pay the Assyrians back for all of their atrocities. Probably not a flood—he had seen a rainbow recently and was reminded that God would not destroy the world again via water. Maybe fire—like Sodom and Gomorrah. Better, how about an earthquake first? Then a giant hailstorm. Followed by fire from heaven to incinerate all that remained. No one would be left alive, not even a dog or a cat!

Then Jonah could return home a hero. What honors would he receive in the royal court if he could report that Israel's biggest problem was solved? He would love to deliver that message: "Good news, your highness—you don't need to worry about Nineveh anymore!"

Something checked Jonah's spirit. There was another possibility. The Ninevites might actually listen to Jonah's preaching. What if they repented? Jonah knew how God worked. God could change His mind and spare the Assyrians. How would Jonah explain *that* to King Jeroboam? "Your highness, I preached to the Ninevites, and they repented and said they would terrorize us no more." Right! The royal court would mock him and accuse him of treason. Aiding and abetting the enemy.

He would have to convince the king and his royal advisers that this was God's doing, not his. God was responsible. God had rescued him from the storm and from the belly of the fish. Wait a minute: That meant God could protect him from the wrath of Israel's king. Suddenly, he did not feel any fear. Nothing the king did to him could be worse than what he had already experienced inside that fish.

For Reflection

What would you like to see happen to your enemies?
Be specific. They could be neighbors or co-workers or
proponents of another political cause. Do you think if
they heard the message that God loves them, they might
behave differently? Who will deliver that message?

2

Operation Nineveh

> Jonah began by going a day's journey into the city, proclaiming,
> "Forty more days and Nineveh will be overturned."
>
> Jonah 3:4 NIV

The sun was going down. People were heading home. A crowd pressed toward the gate. At dark, the city gates were closed, and the surrounding area was not exactly the safest place on earth. Better be inside the walls. That was bad enough.

Among the exhausted workers arriving from their fields walked Jonah. He looked sun-burned, worn and haggard, and his dirty clothing had a peculiar smell to it. You would not want to sit next to him in a crowded restaurant. Or in church!

He had probably lost his eyebrows and beard and much of his hair. His skin was waxy white, as though someone had poured acid over him. Come to think of it, had he not recently spent three days bathing in the stomach acid of a fish? So at the end of the day, Jonah snuck into the great city, trying to avoid attention. This was no time to start preaching.

He found an inn. He had a long, restless night. His thoughts churned inside him while his body turned over and over again until he longed for daybreak. But that would not bring him relief. He was dreading this day.

———

<u>Day One of Operation Nineveh</u>. Jonah decided he would start preaching at the souk. That was the marketplace where surrounding farmers came to sell their lettuce, onions, garlic, eggs, sheep and cattle, wool, leather and cloth. The souk had two distinct advantages. First, a lot of people were gathered there, natives and visitors, so that in one public appearance many would see him. Well, at least from the outside—what his inside, his heart, was like . . . hopefully they would never find out.

Second, it was terribly busy. There were so many voices of merchants shouting who were trying to sell their goods by outshouting their competitors, not to mention those noisy animals. Although there was a maximum of exposure, probably not many would listen.

There was a third advantage to the souk. They sold spices. He established his "pulpit" near that part of the market so that the scents of cinnamon, dill and saffron, along with frankincense, myrrh and nard, would cover up his odor.

Jonah fulfilled his part of the deal: Day one was accomplished. Thirty-nine more to go.

As he walked away from the market, he saw a little girl standing in a doorway clutching a ragged wool doll and staring at him. Behind the girl was her mother. Also staring at him. With tears streaming down her face.

<u>Day Seven of Operation Nineveh</u>. The Sabbath. Glory hallelujah! Jonah had never felt happier with the fourth commandment than on this day. He had no intention of breaking God's holy law. Of the law of love he had not yet heard.

Or had he? What was that again in Exodus 34:6? "The LORD . . . abounding in steadfast love." Away with it! No one can tamper with the Ten Commandments when they are so clear. If today his calf or goat or even his favorite dog would fall into the well, Jonah would not—and I repeat—he would *not* pull the poor creature out of the water. On the Sabbath you do not work. Period!

The people, some of them at least, missed him. He had become kind of familiar to them—that odd man with the bleached skin, no hair and a frightening message.

What did they know about the Jewish religion anyway, much less about the Sabbath? Well, everyone seemed to have a "back to normal" day, almost. There was just a tiny, little nagging doubt in Jonah's heart. Today people here would die, and no one would tell them.

Never had a day off seemed so long and restless to the prophet of God. Even some people in the city thought it was a long day. The little girl with the doll stopped crying. And her mother thought all day about the odd man's message.

For Reflection

Does God want you to deliver His message today?
Where will you take it? When will you begin?

3

It's a Miracle!

The people of Nineveh believed God. They called for a fast and put on sackcloth, from the greatest of them to the least of them.

Jonah 3:5

The word reached the king of Nineveh, and he arose from his throne, removed his robe, covered himself with sackcloth, and sat in ashes.

Jonah 3:6

Word about the strange prophet spread. People who heard him at the souk went home and told their families and neighbors.

Meanwhile Jonah advanced through the huge city. Anywhere he found a noisy crowd, he stopped to deliver his message.

"Thirty more days and Nineveh will be destroyed."

"Twenty more days and Nineveh will be destroyed."

"Ten more days . . ."

Jonah had no program. All he did was preach the Word God gave him. And an amazing thing happened. People stopped to listen to the stranger. Then they started talking.

"Suppose what he says is true?" said one.

"I think he really means it," said another.

"Maybe we'd better do something."

"Maybe *I'd* better do something."

Perhaps that woman and her daughter with the rag doll were the first to grab some burlap bags from the souk. Her husband and neighbors quickly followed their example. Right there by the marketplace where Jonah preached his first message, they put on their sackcloth and sat in front of their homes.

"What are you doing?" one of the merchants asked.

"Didn't you hear the prophet?" the woman said.

"You mean that crazy man with the bleached skin?"

"That man isn't crazy. He said our city would be destroyed. I tell you, God is judging us and we deserve it. We need to pray urgently. I'm dressing in burlap to demonstrate we are truly sorry for our wickedness."

Soon many others were making the sackcloth fashion statement. This was real repentance. They were confessing their sins and calling on God to forgive them. It was a miracle!

The people who heard Jonah preach told everyone they knew. Some of them worked in the palace. They told the servants, who talked with the guards. One of the guards told his captain who reported this to the head of security. The head of security told it to one of the king's advisers, who passed it along to the entire cabinet. The king saw his ministers discussing the situation and wanted to know what they were talking about.

God gave us a message: His Word. It is so strong that a person who responds is transformed from being an alcoholic, a drug addict or a criminal. Or a terrorist.

The drug addict: free.

The alcoholic: delivered.

The criminal: converted.

If we effectively reach people as Jonah did, the fundamentalists of Hinduism or atheism, the Taliban or al Qaeda can become peaceful followers of Jesus.

Then peace can come to the city, the land, the world.

People often comment on how brave I am to go and meet with leaders of terrorist groups and tell them about Jesus. I disagree. That does not require courage. Only obedience! There is nothing I have done that you or anyone could not have done or said or believed. I have often said that if I, a simple Dutchman, can go and do this, then a million people can do it.

We need to get God's message out today. Everyone needs to hear it. Do we really believe God can work that way today? Why not?

We live in a troubled world. War. Hunger. Pandemics. Natural disasters. Persecution. Racism. Crime. Religious fundamentalism. Suicide bombers.

The Bible says that the real underlying problem is *sin*. God did something about sin. The prophets proclaimed that a dire situation can change *if* people will believe and act on their message. If we repent, if we believe God's Word, we could see the miracle of Nineveh repeated today.

The apostle Paul wrote: "It pleased God through the folly of what we preach to save those who believe" (1 Corinthians 1:21).

Something happens when people hear the Word of God. The totally lost can be totally saved because of the perfect Savior.

We who preach the Gospel are the most effective instruments to fight terrorism in the world. Forgiven people are changed people, and they do not blow other people up.

For Reflection

Do you believe God can still drastically change hearts today? Do you really want Him to? Why or why not?

Losing Face

When God saw what they did, how they turned from their evil way, God relented of the disaster that he had said he would do to them, and he did not do it.

Jonah 3:10

But it displeased Jonah exceedingly, and he was angry.

Jonah 4:1

Jonah is moving toward the east gate. There a road leads up the hill. He arrived forty days ago at the west gate. Now his mission is finished. Operation Nineveh is . . . a failure!

God saw what the people of Nineveh did. He saw their sincere repentance. So God did not destroy Nineveh.

In the Middle East, nothing is worse than losing face. That was Jonah's problem. God made him look like a fool. Jonah's prophecy did not come true. After forty days Nineveh remained standing. The people were not cursing—they were singing. They visibly changed, so God changed His mind.

Surely this is one of the greatest miracles of history. Would you not be excited if you preached one sermon and an entire city repented, crime was eliminated and the terrorist threat to your nation no longer existed?

Who is preaching that sermon today?

Maybe we need to pray. Is there a harvest of souls in the Muslim world? Among the Hindu extremists in India? In Communist countries like China and North Korea? In broken nations racked by civil war like Libya and Yemen? If so, we should "ask the Lord of the harvest, therefore, to send out workers into his harvest field" (Matthew 9:38 NIV).

There is a story about a teacher who asked her Sunday school class, "Who wants to go to heaven?" Little Johnny immediately raised his hand. When the teacher recognized him, he answered, "I want to go to heaven, but not with this bunch."

I think that was Jonah's sentiment. It is day 41. The day after Nineveh should have disappeared from the face of the earth. Apparently, God has saved these people that Jonah hated. Did that mean he was going to have to spend eternity with this bunch of heathens?

God is interested in the "day before the day after." Because of what happened the day before, God did not fulfill His threat. Jonah should not have been surprised. He knew what the people of Nineveh did not, that the Lord Almighty had revealed Himself to Moses as "merciful and gracious, slow to anger, and abounding in steadfast love and faithfulness, keeping steadfast love for thousands, forgiving iniquity and transgression and sin, but who will by no means clear the guilty" (Exodus 34:6–7).

If you would only memorize and remember *this* verse, it would be a guiding light in life, helping you to love God and accept His forgiveness. Then you would believe that God can change and save not only your loved ones but also your adversaries!

That was Jonah's problem. He refused to believe that God could save terrorists and transform extremists into peace-loving pacifists.

Maybe you can relate. Maybe you are angry about abortion providers. Or the world's polluters. Or the ultra-opposite wing of the political spectrum from you. Can God really save those folks?

Yes, Jonah was very angry, and he did not mind saying so. His anger was based on what he knew about God. He knew God is gracious, merciful and slow to anger. That does not mean God cannot also be angry. God's anger is specifically mentioned 177 times in the Bible! By contrast, human anger is only mentioned 45 times. God has a lot more reason to be angry than we do.

Jonah is angry because God's love is manifested in an enemy city. "Look at my own country!" Jonah could protest. "Why do I see miracles in a heathen land and not at home? How can you save Nineveh while Israel goes to hell? Is it right that I preach to a non-covenant people and You save them, whereas I preach in Israel and they do not get saved?"

In our home countries we also have unbelief manifesting itself in broken families, collapsed morals, violence and crime on the streets. One mother's son is on drugs. Another man's wife is an alcoholic. A Christian businessman goes broke because his partner stole company funds. Government officials are corrupt. Television broadcasts a steady stream of immoral content. Yet You save Nineveh, God? Why? That is not fair! How can You do that?

God's answer: The people of Nineveh *did* something! They met My conditions. They repented, *all* of them. They turned from their evil ways. And they did not wait until the last day to do it.

For Reflection

Where are the places in your life in which you are concerned about losing face? It may be in your family, or in your politics, your church or your Bible study group.

5

Whose Side Are You On?

He prayed to the LORD and said, "O LORD, is not this what I said when I was yet in my country? That is why I made haste to flee to Tarshish; for I knew that you are a gracious God and merciful, slow to anger and abounding in steadfast love, and relenting from disaster. Therefore now, O LORD, please take my life from me, for it is better for me to die than to live." And the LORD said, "Do you do well to be angry?"

Jonah 4:2–4

Jonah preached judgment to Nineveh. We love to condemn our enemies. Isn't that why there is so much war? We are

219

determined to fight "God's wars," and we are convinced that God is on our side.

Let's not be so sure that we are on God's side. If we truly aligned with God, we would be witnesses to all the world for Jesus Christ.

From the start, Jonah suspected what God would do with Nineveh. Jonah knew that if he preached the word of God, Nineveh might repent. Then God would be gracious, and He would forgive. That is why he ran away from God.

How did Jonah know? It was in his Bible. Jonah's prayer sounds amazingly similar to the revelation of God to Moses in Exodus 34:6–7. Jonah knew about God because he knew God's Book.

If we know God and love God, then we will . . .

know His Book
love His Book
obey His Book

Obedience is not automatic. Jonah knew the Book, but he still argued with God. We need to strive to understand God and His Book. The amazing thing is that God is so patient with Jonah. Jonah can argue with God, and God does not condemn him.

God has a solution for every problem. Jonah has a problem for every solution. Jonah, for example, hates the Assyrians even after they repent. He refuses to give up his hate. God, however, loves Nineveh. He will not let a person, a nation, the world go to hell without a warning. Jonah's problem: He does not want to provide the warning.

To save the world, God sent His Son to die. Jonah would rather die than see Nineveh saved.

Jonah has a problem with God's plan for salvation. Jonah's plan includes only the Jews. God's plan includes Jews *and* their enemies. "Is God the God of the Jews only? Is he not the God of Gentiles also? Yes, of Gentiles also" (Romans 3:29). So God's claim on Nineveh is as strong as His claim on Jerusalem.

How do we get rid of hatred? Jesus said to love your enemies. Because if you love them, they are no longer your enemies. Simple!

Jonah does not want to preach to his enemies. When he is forced to do so, he refuses to love them. In essence he tells God, "You can't make me love them!"

God forgives Nineveh. Jonah does not want them forgiven; he wants them judged.

God has a question for Jonah: "Have you any right to be angry?" Jonah does not answer God. He walks away.

God is telling us, "I have only one plan for the world. That plan includes Nineveh. I only have one message. It is a message of love and of judgment on those who refuse to believe." God says, "I am sending people out into the world to invite all the nations: including Syria, North Korea, Iraq, Iran, China, Russia, Afghanistan and Saudi Arabia. Do not forget America, the Netherlands, the United Kingdom, etc."

"Jonah, if you will not go to Nineveh because they are your enemies, then I have no alternative. You are My plan A and My plan B."

This is so important that Jesus made it His final command: Go into all the world!

God's thinking is so much bigger than ours. We still have not realized how great this salvation is, for us and for the world. We ought to shout it from every roof top!

In my Dutch language translation of the Bible, Jesus tells the disciples that He *had* to suffer, He *had* to rise from the dead on the third day and repentance and remission of sin *had* to be preached in His name to all nations, beginning at Jerusalem (see Luke 24:46–47).

If you leave out any nation, you upset the balance. People will turn to other religions and other gods. Even God cannot save anyone outside of Jesus.

For Reflection

"Know His Book, love His Book, obey His Book." Which of these do you need to work on? How will you begin?

6

A Very Long Wait

Jonah went out of the city and sat to the east of the city and made a booth for himself there. He sat under it in the shade, till he should see what would become of the city.

Jonah 4:5

Jonah sits east of the city, just in case. Why east? He wants to see the sun set on Nineveh. He wants God to keep His promise—all right, fulfill His threat—and destroy the city. Then Jonah's thirst for revenge would be fulfilled. Plus, the threat of the Assyrians to his beloved homeland would be removed. Literally!

223

After all Jonah had been through, after forty days of preaching, after the greatest revival in history with the entire city repenting in sackcloth and ashes, should not Jonah have gone out the west gate? Why west? So he could see the sun rise on a new Nineveh. A Nineveh that was no longer wicked. A Nineveh that was no longer a threat to his beloved homeland. Imagine going home and telling his king that the problem of the Assyrians was solved. That is right! The terrorist threat was gone!

Jonah did not really want a solution. He wanted revenge. He wanted total annihilation. He wanted proof that Nineveh would no longer threaten his people, and what better proof could there be than a black hole where the great city had once been?

Jonah is going to wait a long time. God is not going to change His mind. Because He *already* changed His mind. He will not execute judgment on Nineveh because Nineveh met His conditions for salvation and protection.

When any person or group meets God's conditions, they are automatically entitled to God's protection.

Repentance means we go back to God's rules. We simply need to fit into God's plan to become participants in His power. "Righteousness exalts a nation" (Proverbs 14:34), not just an individual.

How long is Jonah prepared to wait? He is still going to be waiting when he is ready for a retirement home. Jonah is waiting—for a negative. God is acting—on a positive.

I wonder, are we any more interested in real solutions to today's conflicts? God's solution: changed lives. The world's answer: bullets and bombs. Which one is more powerful?

President Lincoln was once asked why he spoke some kind words about his enemies when he should destroy them. Lincoln responded, "Do I not destroy my enemies when I make them my friends?"[1]

Some of my Christian friends have criticized me for going to terrorists in Gaza. They protest: How can I talk with Israel's enemies? My answer: The best thing I can do for Israel is to win her enemies to Christ.

Why do we have so little faith? We complain that God does not answer prayer. God says He wants to answer our prayers for people to be saved, and that miracles would follow our faith. Jonah did not even pray for the salvation of Nineveh. Imagine the joy if he had—God was prepared to answer that prayer. He answered it anyway!

So Jonah, do you have any right to be angry? You have only the right to obey. Leave the rest to Me.

Jonah did not answer God's question. Disobedience has no answer. Except to sulk and run away. God's love for Nineveh is evidence of His desire and ability to save *every* hostile city and nation. God can save Baghdad and Kabul. He can save Amsterdam and London. He can save Detroit and Las Vegas.

Jonah is very far from the example of Jesus. "A body have you prepared for me," Jesus said. "Behold, I have come to do your will, O God" (Hebrews 10:5, 7).

Following the example of Jesus, God has prepared a body. Jonah's body. My body. Your body. Look in the mirror. God has prepared *you*! To do what? To seek and to save the *lost*.

The story of Nineveh should encourage us. If God can save Nineveh, He can save any city. If God has done something on which the salvation of the whole world depends, and if I know it, then I have no choice. I must proclaim it, live for it, suffer for it. Even be willing to die for it.

In heaven, I would rather be told off for loving too much than for loving too little.

For Reflection

Who are the enemies in your life who need to become your friends? If there is compassion in your heart, how is it demonstrated to the world? If there is none, what will it take for you to have compassion for the lost of the world?

Initial Success

> But Pharaoh said, "Who is the LORD, that I should obey his voice and let Israel go?"
>
> Exodus 5:2

Forty years after running away, Moses returned to Egypt. He connected with Aaron, and together they met with the elders of Israel. Aaron spoke the words Moses gave him. They performed the signs. And the people believed!

What a great start! If Moses was a missionary writing home to his supporters, he would eagerly report on the favor he had received and how the elders had bowed their heads and worshiped God (see Exodus 4:31). The first big hurdle was overcome. Moses and Aaron were ready to advance to phase two: an audience with Pharaoh. Moses would no doubt urge his supporters to pray about this meeting.

With confidence, the pair delivered God's message: "Let My people go" (Exodus 5:1). Pharaoh was convicted, agreed that he had abused God's people and repented of his wicked ways.

"Wait a minute!" you protest. "That is *not* what happened." But is that not what we expect when we follow God's directions? Surely everything should work out according to our plans. In spiritual battle, of course, that rarely happens. The enemy is also at work, and his puppets (they probably do not realize they are under demonic influence) are going to resist God's agenda.

If we have learned anything from Jonah and Nineveh, we know that the Egyptians could have repented had Pharaoh led the way. There is always the possibility for repentance.

Sadly, Egypt's monarch revealed his true nature by challenging God. "Who is the LORD, that I should obey his voice? . . . I do not know the LORD, and moreover, I will not let Israel go" (verse 2). So Pharaoh threw down the gauntlet. God had warned Moses that He would harden Pharaoh's heart. Now we see it.

From there, the situation deteriorated. The ruler made life miserable for the Hebrews. He demanded more work from the slaves—because obviously they did not have enough to do if they wanted to take a holiday under religious pretext. So the people suffered.

We tend to assume that things will "go right" if we follow God's leading. That clearly did not happen with Moses. In fact, his problems increased. Slave masters demanded more work out of the Hebrews and stopped providing the straw they needed to make the bricks for Pharaoh's massive building program. The people turned on Moses. They said, in essence, "It's all your fault! We were doing okay until you came along. (They weren't really.) Now look at what you've done."

When times get tough, do not expect everyone to understand and sympathize with you. Often Christians say the meanest things. They are quick to accuse that you have not really followed God's lead because if you had, this disaster would not be happening.

Moses could very well have argued with the people. He could have told them to hold tight—God has promised to free us, and we just have to be patient. He could have reminded them of the stories of Abraham, Isaac and Jacob and the trials they experienced as they followed God. Or of Joseph, who suffered slavery and imprisonment for a dozen years before advancing to Number Two Man in Egypt and saving Israel. He could have told them how God had foretold that this would happen—we cannot expect Pharaoh to just sit back and let us leave, depleting his cheap workforce.

This is where spiritual warfare becomes a serious challenge. Obedience never guarantees a smooth path because the forces of evil and hell never cooperate with God's plan. Jesus warned us, "If the world hates you, know that it has hated me before it hated you" (John 15:18). We should not be surprised by opposition. Yet it seems we often are.

Do we give up when opposition arises or increases? It is natural to recoil when facing hatred. We must focus on the calling of God and realize that His promises will come true—in His timing. Moses was only starting His work. Soon God would reveal just how powerful He is.

For Reflection

Have you seen things "go wrong" by obeying God? Did you give up or persevere? Why?

2

Don't Expect a Pat
on the Back

[The foremen of the people of Israel] said to [Moses and
Aaron], "The LORD look on you and judge, because you have
made us stink in the sight of Pharaoh and his servants, and
have put a sword in their hand to kill us."

Exodus 5:21

Moses did not try to convince the people of the rightness of
his action. He did not urge them to focus on the promise of
freedom. He did not defend himself or God. Instead, Moses
turned to the Lord and spoke frankly. "Why have you done

evil to this people? Why did you ever send me? For since I came to Pharaoh to speak in your name, he has done evil to this people, and you have not delivered your people at all" (Exodus 5:22–23).

Translation: What is taking so long? Things have gotten much worse and, God, it is all Your fault!

Ever felt that way? Most of us have.

The beauty of Moses is that he expressed his frustrations in the right place. These were not polite words. He accused God of doing evil (some translations soften that prayer—instead asking God why he has brought this trouble on the people). We do not need to be cautious when speaking our hearts to God. He knows our thoughts already, so why not be honest? Moses was frank, and God did not rebuke him.

This was God's reply: "Now you shall see what I will do to Pharaoh" (Exodus 6:1). Hang on, Moses. Now the real fun begins! Then God reminded Moses of something He did not give Abraham or Isaac or Jacob—His name. That is significant. He recalled His covenant with the patriarchs to give the people the land of Canaan. He repeated that He had heard the groaning of the people—He understood their suffering—and He had promised to deliver the people from slavery and to do so with great acts of judgment. Then He would bring them to the Promised Land, deliver it to them and be their God.

There is a lot here. It is a reminder of how we need to continually—daily, actually—hear God's instructions and promises to us. Are you committed to spending time every day feeding your mind with Scripture?

Moses was revived by the words from God. Finally, he was able to face the people. With God's clear message, he spoke to the people of Israel to assure them that all would come to pass as promised.

Did the people respond positively to God's message? They did *not* listen. They were frustrated and discouraged. Moses was all alone. No one was following him. That is tough for a leader. Would Moses persevere in the face of such disappointment?

Here is the challenge. The people Moses is supposedly leading are dejected. Actually, it is worse. Their spirits are broken. God tells Moses to go back to Pharaoh and repeat the demand to let the Hebrews go. Moses answers by saying, in essence, "What's the point?" The people of Israel have not listened to him. Why should Pharaoh listen to him? So far, God's plan feels like a disaster.

Then God makes an amazing statement to Moses. One that should grab our attention and shake us to the core. "See, I have made you like God to Pharaoh" (Exodus 7:1).

I am sure Moses does not feel like God to anyone. That does not matter. Regardless of how he feels, it is a fact. This is vitally important because the king must learn who Yahweh, the one true God, is. He must know Who is behind all the disasters that will soon befall his kingdom. How will he learn? The only way he can is through another person who knows God personally.

What makes this more poignant is that Pharaoh is supposedly god in Egypt; therefore, a confrontation is inevitable. Human god will meet the real God and learn who is more powerful. That is the drama behind the ten plagues that occupy chapters 7 through 12 of Exodus.

There is additional significance. If Moses is like God to Pharaoh, then Moses is untouchable. Is it not likely that the king wanted to kill Moses? This man was a threat to Egypt's economy and security. The obvious solution was to eliminate the leader of this rebellion. But Pharaoh cannot touch God's man. God will not allow it.

When you follow God's directions, you are protected until such time as your mission is accomplished. That does not mean it is safe. It was dangerous to deliver and repeat an unwanted message to an obstinate tyrant. Still, God is responsible for our protection while we fulfill His mandate. Is it possible that we may not return? Yes, it is possible. Go anyway! Go with confidence because you are on a divine mission.

For Reflection

How do you respond when your expectations of God are not met? What is your plan to daily hear from God through reading your Bible and to gain the direction, encouragement and strength you need?

3

This Is War!

So Moses and Aaron went to Pharaoh and did just as the LORD commanded.

Exodus 7:10

The magicians said to Pharaoh, "This is the finger of God." But Pharaoh's heart was hardened, and he would not listen to them, as the LORD had said.

Exodus 8:19

Let the battle begin! The gods of Egypt versus the Creator of the universe. The so-called god Pharaoh versus the God of Moses. A pantheon of deities versus Yahweh, the great I AM.

By nature, most of us avoid conflict. We prefer compromise. Peace at almost any cost. Moses, however, at God's instigation, embraced confrontation. Pharaoh had real power, which included the occult. When Aaron threw down his staff and it became a serpent, the king called on his magicians, and they duplicated the feat. Then Aaron's staff swallowed up the magicians' staffs. That show did not convince Pharaoh of God's superior power. It would take much more to change his mind.

The first plague, changing the water of the Nile into blood, Pharaoh's magicians duplicated by their secret arts. The second plague, calling up the frogs, was likewise matched by the conjurers, although those men could not end the frog problem—Pharaoh needed Moses to pray to Yahweh for that to happen.

The third plague revealed the limit of human tricks. The magicians could not turn dust into gnats, and they admitted to Pharaoh, "This is the finger of God." Pharaoh paid no attention.

Thus, the war escalated—the powers of the occult, political might and God Himself collided. People suffered as a result. They endured boils, crops were destroyed and their livestock was wiped out. Did the people of Egypt realize the spiritual significance of these events? Probably not. They just suffered.

Never enter into spiritual combat lightly. We must engage the enemy only under the direction and protection of God because victory by human means is impossible.

I must emphasize this point. You are incapable of prevailing in spiritual conflict *unless* God directs you and provides you with His resources.

It is essential to remember that on their own, Moses and Aaron could not perform a single miracle. They had no ability to defeat the gods of Egypt unless God Himself acted. They simply followed God's orders.

Do not think the confrontation between God and Pharaoh was a unique event. Like Moses, we are called to be God's instruments in spiritual combat.

Jesus, however, expects us to confront the powers of this world while remembering always that He said, "Apart from me you can do nothing" (John 15:5). We depend on being connected to the vine, the person of Christ. We must be controlled by the Holy Spirit.

In addition, we can call on the Father in prayer and ask for any resources we need to accomplish His Son's mission. Jesus said if we believed in Him, we would do the works He did, and greater works. That is impossible! No, it is not. "Whatever you ask in my name, this I will do, that the Father may be glorified in the Son. If you ask me anything in my name, I will do it" (John 14:13–14).

Paul the apostle never shunned a confrontation with the occult. Paul and Barnabas were in Cyprus and met a false prophet, a sorcerer named Elymas, who had influence with the governor (see Acts 13:4–12). The governor wanted to hear the word of God from Barnabas and Paul, but Elymas interfered and urged the governor to ignore the Gospel. Luke, the author of Acts, emphasized that Paul was full of the Holy Spirit. He called the false prophet "son of the devil," and exposed him as a fraud. Then Paul declared the deceiver would be struck blind, and immediately Elymas began groping in darkness. The governor became a believer.

We need that kind of Spirit-inspired boldness today. Yes, the spiritual forces in the world are strong. Never minimize them. Occultism is widespread and we should naturally be wary of it; however, it must be confronted. If we are convinced something is evil, why do we not say it?

If you know God, there is no need to fear the enemy. The gates of hell cannot withstand the power of the resurrected Christ.

For Reflection

Where do you see evidence of spiritual warfare in the world? Is there a part you are called to play in the spiritual conflict around you? How will you recognize the leading of the Holy Spirit in the battle?

4

A Prayer Battle

The LORD said to Moses, "Go down, for your people, whom you brought up out of the land of Egypt, have corrupted themselves."

Exodus 32:7

Moses implored the LORD his God.

Exodus 32:11

Moses and God are having a delightful time. True, Moses is fasting, but he is not focused on his body. For days God has revealed plans for an exquisite tabernacle where the people of Israel can meet Him. Moses has captured every detail—all the measurements and blueprints for each piece of furniture.

Suddenly God disowns the Hebrews. These are not His people anymore. What could produce such outrage? God spells it out:

- The people have turned aside from the way that I commanded them.
- They have made for themselves a golden calf and have worshiped it.
- They have said, "These are your gods, O Israel, who brought you up out of the land of Egypt."
- The Hebrews are a stiff-necked people.

What Moses heard next absolutely rocked him. "Leave Me alone. I am so angry that I will destroy them all. I am going to start over. Moses, I will make a great nation out of you" (Exodus 32:10, paraphrase).

Has anyone ever had an offer like that? Maybe Noah—God wiped out the whole world and started over with one family. If He did it before, He could do it again. As Creator, He certainly possessed that right.

God's declaration, however, presented Moses with a dilemma. Here was his big chance to escape the job of leading a bunch of ingrates and infidels who turned their backs on God at every opportunity. The slate could be wiped clean, and he could become the patriarch of a great nation. How many of us could say no to such an offer?

Moses had acted on principle when he left Pharaoh's palace and chose to align himself with the Hebrews. How could he turn his back on these people now? If Moses could just calm God down—how does anyone do that?—maybe he could present another perspective. That sounds crazy but it is what Moses was thinking.

God feels betrayed. The Hebrews are attempting a *coup d'état.* It has been barely three months since God miraculously rescued the Hebrews. Now they say a blob of metal rescued them. What an insult! God's honor has been shamed. In the Middle East, then and now, such shame cannot be ignored.

This is a major crisis in the history of Israel, and the people have no clue that their future is at stake. Moses takes responsibility by saying, in essence, "God, You can't do this!" Moses does not accept a word from God as the Word of God. Not yet anyway. Not without some serious intercession.

Various translations of Exodus 32:11 say, "Moses sought the favor of the LORD" (NIV), "Moses implored the LORD his God" (ESV), "Moses entreated the LORD his God" (NASB), "Moses tried to pacify the LORD his God" (NLT), and "Moses tried to calm his GOD down" (MSG).

All of those translations feel too tame. In God's current state, nothing Moses says will make a difference. I combed lexicons and commentaries and learned that the Hebrew verb conveys the idea of someone touching or, more accurately, massaging. The picture is of Moses reaching out and caressing the face of God.

We could argue, of course, that Moses could not literally see or touch God's face. Later we learn that Moses met with God face-to-face as with a friend (see Exodus 33:11). Still later, Moses wants to see God's glory and God insists that no one can see His face and live. What is actually happening? Without many details, we know Moses and God are in close proximity. We do not know what Moses actually sees. Still, somehow, Moses attempts to calm an angry God so that he might speak words that would save his people.

Certainly, Moses has reason to feel frustration with the Hebrews. Nevertheless, they *are* his people. That was settled more than forty years ago when he chose to identify with the Hebrews and reject the life of royalty in Pharaoh's palace. Does Moses throw away his investment? He cannot! But how does anyone reason with an angry God?

This is where Moses' most intense battle begins.

For Reflection

Do you agree that Moses was correct to try to calm down God? Why or why not? Have you ever thought that a group of people were so wicked that God should wipe them out? How do you process such thoughts?

5

Can God Really Change His Mind?

Moses implored the LORD his God and said, "O LORD, why does your wrath burn hot against your people?"

Exodus 32:11

So the LORD changed his mind about the terrible disaster he had threatened to bring on his people.

Exodus 32:14 NLT

Moses understood God's compassion—he saw it at his first encounter at the burning bush when God said He had heard

243

the cries of the people. Moses played on that compassion and more. He reminded God that He had brought the people "out of the land of Egypt with great power and with a mighty hand" (Exodus 32:11). Moses was saying, "God, this was Your doing, not mine. I was just Your human instrument."

Then Moses appealed to God's reputation. Why should the Egyptians slander God by saying that He brought them out of the land "to kill them in the mountains and to consume them from the face of the earth?" (verse 12). What goes unsaid is that God had defeated all the gods of Egypt. He had demonstrated favoritism to the Hebrews. All those miracles would go to waste because no one would ever want to associate with Yahweh.

Finally, Moses recalled the promises God had made to Abraham, Isaac and Jacob. "Remember those promises," he says. He calls Yahweh to remember that He said, "I will multiply your offspring as the stars of heaven, and all this land that I have promised I will give to your offspring, and they shall inherit it forever" (verse 13).

So God, are You going to keep Your promise?

Technically, God could fulfill that oath through Moses and still destroy the Hebrews who had turned away from Him. But that certainly was not the spirit of those ancient covenants. Unspoken was the deeper root issue—would the descendants of Moses fare any better?

Based on these arguments, Moses begged God not to carry out His threat to destroy the people. Amazingly, God listened. And God changed His mind.

In spiritual battle we are confronted with this challenge: Are we willing to go toe-to-toe with God and plead for the salvation of people? Are we willing to appeal to Him based on His reputation?

If all we do is pray for personal needs for ourselves and our friends, we will never know God the way Moses did. And we will never make an impact on the world.

In 1990, I (Andrew) wrote a book called *And God Changed His Mind*. Many people objected to that title, arguing that God is unchanging. He chose us before the creation of the world. He knows the beginning and the end. He is omniscient, the author of providence. How could God possibly change His mind?

If that is true, let's surrender to God's will and accept our fate! In fact, why bother to pray at all if everything is predetermined? Maybe Moses should salute and say, "Aye, aye, Lord! Your will be done." Moses did not do that. He passionately attempted to persuade God not to carry out His threats.

Including this crisis, there are at least seven times in the Old Testament when God changed His mind. Some versions translate the Hebrew word as "relented" or some similar word. God revealed to the prophet Amos that He would send a plague of locusts. Amos prayed, "O Sovereign LORD, please forgive us or we will not survive, for Israel is so small" (Amos 7:2 NLT). Later in another vision God revealed that He would punish Israel with a great fire. Again, Amos prayed: "O Sovereign LORD, please stop or we will not survive, for Israel is so small" (verse 5 NLT). Both times "The LORD relented from this plan" and said, "I will not do it" (verses 3, 6 NLT).

Was God toying with Amos? Was this a game? I do not think so.

Observe one more example from the opposite perspective. Through the prophet Ezekiel, God revealed:

> I sought for a man among them who should build up the wall and stand in the breach before me for the land, that I should not destroy it, but I found none. Therefore I have poured out my indignation upon them. I have consumed them with the fire of my wrath.
>
> Ezekiel 22:30–31

Clearly God wanted someone to talk Him out of this judgment. God is omniscient, of course. He is also a person who wants to interact with us. When the stakes are high, we can make a difference. When we do not get involved, people may perish.

For Reflection

Do you believe God can change His mind? Why or why not? What does this tell you about how to pray?

6

History's Boldest Prayer

Then I lay prostrate before the LORD as before, forty days
and forty nights. . . . The LORD listened to me that time also.

Deuteronomy 9:18–19

The next day Moses said to the people, ". . . perhaps I can
make atonement for your sin."

Exodus 32:30

Moses was utterly exhausted. Anyone who has fasted just a
few days knows the feeling. Forty days with no food—Moses
was at the end of his physical resources. Then he had to deal

with the Israelites' apostasy. We do not know how long it was before he went back to appeal to God. Probably not very long because of the urgency of the crisis.

We imagine Moses practically crawling back up the mountain. When he reaches the summit, he is too tired to even sit upright. He falls flat on his face. Rocks dig into his dry skin. Dust covers his hair and beard. Scorpions nibble on his toes. His lips are cracked from lack of moisture. Moses does not care. He has an appeal to make, a proposal that cannot wait. Listen to how Moses pleads with the Almighty Yahweh:

> So I lay prostrate before the LORD for these forty days and forty nights, because the LORD had said he would destroy you. And I prayed to the LORD, "O Lord GOD, do not destroy your people and your heritage, whom you have redeemed through your greatness, whom you have brought out of Egypt with a mighty hand."
>
> Deuteronomy 9:25–26

That is serious prayer! There are commentators who would say God never intended to carry out the destruction of the Hebrews. This was a test to see what Moses would do. You can make that argument, though it rips the heart out of this scene. Moses is convinced that God will carry out a holocaust if he does not intercede for the people.

Moses had already received instructions concerning sacrifices. The details are spelled out in Leviticus. Moses also realized that this sin of idolatry required something bigger than the sacrifice of bulls or goats or pigeons. What could be that greater sacrifice? Not knowing of God's plan to send His Son, Moses can imagine only one possibility. He is not sure, but what if he offered himself? *Maybe I can make atonement.*

So Moses offered the boldest prayer in history. It is the most Christlike prayer possible. Gone is the anger. Moses is now consumed by passion for lost souls and is willing to lay down his own life—not just his physical life, but eternal life as well—if only the people of Israel could be saved.

Talk about guts! Moses takes a gigantic leap of faith. He proposes to do what Jesus will in fact do fourteen hundred years later. He acts and speaks with such perfect insight into God's character and purpose that shortly before Calvary, he will stand with Elijah on the Mount of Transfiguration and talk with Jesus about what His atoning death in Jerusalem will accomplish.

God makes a counterproposal to Moses' offer of atonement. He declares, "Whoever has sinned against me, I will blot out of my book" (Exodus 32:33). A plague was sent among them—we are spared the details. The Israelites paid a high price for their sin. Still, because of Moses' intervention, God did not totally destroy the people.

I have meditated long on the words in Hebrews that say Moses "considered the reproach of Christ greater wealth than the treasures of Egypt" (Hebrews 11:26). Jesus insisted that Moses wrote about Him—"If you believed Moses, you would believe me; for he wrote of me" (John 5:46). I believe this scene is the climactic event when Moses, without realizing it, fully identified with Christ. Here is where Moses demonstrated true love. He was willing to lay down his own life to save his people—just as Jesus was willing to, and actually did, lay down His life to save the world.

If we followers of Christ could employ this kind of prayer, the world would not be the same. When praying for the salvation of individuals, for a nation or for the world, a critical element in our communion with God is our willingness to offer up our very lives. Totally selfless prayer will change a world in need because then it will see the reality of Christ. How else will the lost understand what Christ is like?

For Reflection

Is there a person or group of people you know and care about who are lost? Looking at the example of Moses, how will you pray for them?

Call to Arms

The Spirit of the LORD clothed Gideon, and he sounded the trumpet, and the Abiezrites were called out to follow him.

Judges 6:34

Never go to war alone. You need resources.

Here is the key resource: "The Spirit of the LORD clothed Gideon." That is the secret of spiritual warfare. We must be filled with the Holy Spirit! That is *the* primary resource God provides to fulfill His mission.

At first that sounds like a contradiction to God's introductory call. Gideon was told "Go in your strength." He protests: "But, God, I have no strength. I'm the least of the least." Gideon is spot on; thus, the note here that Gideon is clothed in power and authority. His strength is the Spirit of God.

God provided His Spirit to each of the warriors we have studied. The same was not true of the general population. In the Old Testament, people depended on God's hand-selected, Spirit-directed spokespersons.

Today, as followers of Christ, each of us is gifted with the Holy Spirit. This Spirit brings us peace in the midst of turmoil. He guides us into all truth, using primarily the Word of God in Scripture. The Holy Spirit is the presence of Christ. It is Jesus living in us. This is the life of the vine—Jesus said we should abide in Him, the vine. Apart from this connection we can do . . . well, actually, nothing!

Gideon has the single most critical resource for his assignment—the presence of God that has clothed him; however, the circumstances have not changed. Not one Midianite has been eliminated. In fact, 120,000 of them have crossed the Jordan River and camped in the Valley of Jezreel. At any moment, the Israelites could be attacked, slaughtered and have all of their livelihood destroyed.

That is a terrifying situation. Except for Gideon. He now has a relationship with God. He is clothed with God's Spirit. One fruit of the Spirit is peace. *So Gideon, while everyone around you is in panic mode and no one experiences peace, you remain calm, ready to respond to the direction of God's Spirit.*

That is the confidence we can have as followers of Christ. We have a peace based exclusively on the peace Jesus brought about on the cross. Without the cross of Jesus Christ, we have no message. We must take up our cross daily and follow Him. That is our message in a world that is torn apart. "Peace is knowing the reason not to be frightened by the facts this time."[1]

What Israel wants, what every country needs, is peace. At a time when everyone seems to scream and yell hatred and violence, there is a peace that passes all understanding. You cannot explain it intellectually. You do not need to—it should radiate from your life.

Gideon is ready to advance against Midian. All he needs is—well, a few more soldiers would help. One man against 120,000 is a challenge even for a man clothed with the Spirit of the Lord. Gideon pulls out the family trumpet and blows a blast. The people in his tribe, the Abiezrites, come running. They have seen Gideon boldly remove local idols. Maybe this is someone they can follow. Perhaps God has raised him up to lead them to victory.

The men wait for instructions. This small gathering is a start, but they could use more troops. Gideon points to several men. "You, you and you—go to Manasseh and see how many fighters you can recruit." The Abiezrites are a subtribe of Manasseh. Family.

Gideon calls for more messengers. They spread out and recruit men from the tribes of Asher, Zebulun and Naphtali. Finally, Gideon assembles the semblance of an army. They are still greatly outnumbered. But at least hope is kindled.

There is not one problem that is too big in your life, in your community, in your nation that God cannot solve through His presence. He then provides the resources you need, including brothers and sisters to battle alongside you. To Gideon, it becomes clear that God is his deliverance, his rescue, his peace.

For Reflection

Consider the problem you are facing in your home or in your culture. Are you experiencing the peace God promises? Why or why not? Do you have a support team, one or a few people who will provide encouragement and prayer support?

Who's on the Team?

The LORD said to Gideon, "The people with you are too many for me to give the Midianites into their hand, lest Israel boast over me, saying, 'My own hand has saved me.'"

Judges 7:2

In warfare, numbers matter. It is not that a smaller army cannot win with better tactics. It certainly can. Still, the greater the numerical and material advantage, the better the odds that an army can defeat the enemy.

So how great of an army does Israel need to win this war? Gideon gathers his soldiers and brings them to the spring at Harod, which was a short distance to the north and where the

Midianite force camped. Now what? Let's organize. Maybe appoint some lieutenants and sergeants? Then train the men. And develop a strategy. That is how I would manage this.

Fortunately, Gideon still has an ear tuned to God, and he gets instructions that must have stunned him. *You have too many men.*

How will Gideon respond? Does Gideon see this as his big opportunity to move up in the world? Is he positioning himself to gain national attention as a military genius that he can parlay into financial and political power? If that is his thinking, God quickly reminds him who is in charge. This is not Israel's or even Gideon's moment to shine. God is going to crush the enemy, and He will get the glory.

So, pare down the army. But how? Should Gideon conduct physical exams to see who is in the best shape? Maybe they need a skills test— select the best archers; dismiss those who cannot handle a sword. God said, "Let the individuals themselves decide. Anyone who is afraid and trembling, leave now. Go home!"

If Gideon knew his Bible, he would recall Deuteronomy 20:8: "The officers shall speak further to the people, and say, 'Is there any man who is fearful and fainthearted?' Let him go back to his house, lest he make the heart of his fellows melt like his own." It is quite simple: Fear is infectious. The problem with fearful soldiers is that they talk. That is also true of fearful missionaries.

A man I deeply admire, Nik Ripken, has done some of the most significant research into what makes for effective missions. Along the way, he discovered that the primary concern of Western missionaries is safety. "It may be time for the church in the West to admit that we are afraid," Nik writes.

Often when MBBs (Muslim Background Believers) are asked what they learn from missionaries they sadly respond with, "Missionaries teach us to be afraid." This is not just a missiological mistake. It is a sin. They expound that missionaries are afraid of getting local believers arrested or harmed. They are afraid they will lose their visa or work permit. They fear moving, learning yet another language or placing their children in yet another school. Where did missionaries learn to be afraid?

Nik concludes, "Fear is devastating. It paralyses. It causes one to run when no one is chasing. Fear is a black hole, an abyss, which will suck the joy from the soul of a believer."[1]

When the fearful men are excused, 22,000 men clear out. Shocking! Israel is in bad shape, and the reason is that they have not made Yahweh their God. The solution to fear is that God's love casts out fear. There are far too many Christians who know nothing of God's love. They are excused before the battle starts.

Now the odds for Gideon and Israel are twelve to one. None of the Midianites have gone home and only 10,000 soldiers remain. Yet God is not done. There are still too many!

It is not up to Gideon to winnow the number. God is selecting Gideon's team, his army. Gideon is ordered to take the men down to the stream where they will be tested. God will reveal His choices to Gideon.

There were two types of men who drank at the stream. One group knelt down to drink. The other group scooped up water and put their hands to their mouths. Those were the ones God chose. Just three hundred total!

The Lord concludes, "With these 300 men I will rescue you and give you victory over the Midianites" (Judges 7:7 NLT). What should the other 9,700 do? They can pray! And participate in the mop-up operation.

For Reflection

Has God given you a team? How were they selected? How do you know that they are the ones God has selected for you and your mission?

3

Sure I'm Scared

That same night the LORD said to him, ". . . If you are afraid to go down, go down to the camp with Purah your servant. And you shall hear what they say, and afterward your hands shall be strengthened."

Judges 7:9–11

People ask me all the time if I get scared. I have gone multiple times to Lebanon during their civil war. I have tried to sleep nights in Gaza while gunfire rattled in the streets. When I watch the news, I fear for those brothers and sisters caught in war or natural disaster or riots or persecution. So yes, I am scared all the time. *I go anyway.*

If you are never afraid, then you have no courage. I have the same view of doubt. Faith without doubt is not faith.

When we see what is happening in the world, we should fear—fear that unless God takes over, we are doomed. In such circumstances, we need encouragement. It is interesting that Gideon did not ask for this final sign. God gave it anyway. Probably Gideon needed it. Or maybe God just wanted to give it.

The encouragement Gideon receives comes from an incredible source. He is led to go down to the camp with his servant, Purah. What he saw there was terrifying. It reminded him of a swarm of locusts. Like a plague, this horde had cleaned out Israel's crops year after year. There was no way his little squad of three hundred men could defeat this immense army.

Then he hears a man at the outpost recounting a dream to his comrade. The dream itself was strange. "A cake of barley bread tumbled into the camp of Midian," the man said, "and came to the tent and struck it so that it fell and turned it upside down, so that the tent lay flat" (verse 13).

What in the world could that mean?

The man's companion answered. "This is no other than the sword of Gideon the son of Joash, a man of Israel; God has given into his hand Midian and all the camp" (verse 14).

Really? How does someone get that interpretation from the dream? Unless this is God inspired. Which is exactly how Gideon received it. As soon as he heard the dream and its interpretation, he worshiped. When we are released from fear, we are able to worship almighty God. Then we are ready for battle.

Many times before heading behind the Iron Curtain, or later, traveling to the Middle East, God knew I needed encouragement. On one occasion I was headed to Eastern Europe when, on my way out of Holland, I stopped at a home where I knew a prayer meeting was being held. I shared with the leader about my assignment, and she called the group to gather around me and pray over me. As they prayed, I felt a jolt of energy surge through me—I believe it was the Holy Spirit. I knew then I was ready to proceed.

How does God encourage us today? We can be encouraged by stories of how God is working around the world. I love stories of Muslims who have dreams and visions of Jesus that lead them to find a Christian or receive a Bible. If God can work that way, then He can use me also.

We should also be encouraged by fellow believers who pray for us. When Al teamed up with me in 2001, he was encouraged by Sealy Yates, our board chairman, to develop a prayer team. Sealy assured him that he would be his first prayer partner. Gradually that list grew until there were more than 250 friends and acquaintances around the world on his email list. They prayed for us every time we traveled. Many times, when exhaustion was setting in, we felt a burst of energy. Often later we heard from someone that he or she had been praying for us at that exact moment.

Never go into battle without prayer support. That is often the source of encouragement you need. And the best antidote to fear.

For Reflection

Where can you go to receive encouragement? Do you have a prayer team? If not, you might want to start gathering a few prayer warriors around you.

4

What's the Plan?

As soon as Gideon heard the telling of the dream and its interpretation, he worshiped. And he returned to the camp of Israel and said, "Arise, for the LORD has given the host of Midian into your hand."

Judges 7:15

Gideon is ready to charge into battle. He has heard Yahweh's mission, he has assembled his troops and he has received the encouragement he needs. He is energized. Confident. Victory is assured!

What a difference a relationship with God makes. When the angel of the Lord first appeared to Gideon at Ophrah, he

263

was afraid, working in secret, with no confidence whatsoever. Now, he is transformed and filled with the Spirit and ready for action.

That is all wonderful. But there are three hundred men waiting for instructions. They have not heard what Gideon heard. They need a battle plan. What is the strategy?

Here we see Gideon's creativity. It is bold and imaginative. Scripture does not say that God gave Gideon this specific plan, but he is certainly divinely inspired. He calls the men together and divides them into three teams. He hands out the weapons. Everyone receives one trumpet, an empty jar and a torch.

What kind of weapons are these? How are we supposed to fight? We need swords, or bows and arrows, javelins.

Actually, Gideon understands that the men will not need traditional weapons, at least not initially. If they do have swords, they are strapped to the body. They will carry torches in their left hands and blow the trumpets they hold in their right hands.

It is a dark night. Probably moonless. Most of the Midianites are asleep. Three groups of one hundred advance quietly to the rim of the enemy camp. It is the start of the second watch, around midnight. The sentries are tired, ready to bunk down, and replacements are having a tough time waking up. They need coffee. Besides, they assume no one will attack at this hour.

Gideon has instructed that he will give the signal. With all his men in place, Gideon blows his trumpet. The hundred men with him do the same. The other two groups answer with trumpet salvos. Everyone smashes their jars. The noise is deafening, magnified by the rocky terrain. Then they shout, "A sword for the LORD and for Gideon" (verse 20).

The noise shatters the night. They have unleashed a powerful psychological weapon. The Midianites are sure they are under attack from a huge army. It is dark. No time to light their torches. They scramble for their weapons. They panic. Thinking the enemy is in their camp, they furiously fight each other. Those who are not instantly killed run for their lives. The Israelite soldiers stand fast as the Midianites scatter.

It is an incredible moment. Did God give Gideon these specific instructions? Or did he, clothed with God's Spirit, have divine insight to draft this unique plan? I believe God enables us to use our intellect to fulfill His mission—as long as we remain responsive to His Spirit. God can provide us peace as we make plans. He can also check us in our spirit, prompting us to adjust our strategy. We may listen to advice from others but always with one ear aimed toward heaven. When we are filled with the Holy Spirit, we should be aligned constantly with His direction.

There was only one possible caution in Gideon's plan. The men shouted, "For the Lord." Absolutely correct! This was God's battle. He would fight for them. But they also added the name of their human commander. Why? Gideon was a deputy, not the Commander-in-Chief. This might cause problems later.

Still, this is a glorious night. Certain defeat is turned into glorious victory. Each Israelite soldier stands and watches as the enemy self-destructs. Those who are not killed run. As Paul writes to us today: "Thanks be to God, who gives us the victory through our Lord Jesus Christ" (1 Corinthians 15:57).

The example of Gideon shows us that spiritual warfare is not conducted as the world fights war. The world relies on raw power, intellectual intimidation, large amounts of money and ever-increasing technological innovation.

Our God is far more creative. When He calls us into battle, He equips us with unusual tools. We will likely be understaffed—certainly not in the majority. But filled with His Spirit, we have an advantage. We have weapons that destroy the arguments and lofty opinions of the those the world considers wise (see 2 Corinthians 10:3–5.)

For Reflection

What are some of the weapons God is supplying to you that seem foolish or weak? How might God have you wield those weapons in the spiritual battle facing you?

5

God Gives the Victory

When they blew the 300 trumpets, the LORD set every man's sword against his comrade and against all the army. And the army fled.

Judges 7:22

The battle is won, but the war is not over. Many Midianites die when God causes them to panic and slice each other up with their swords. The survivors run, heading toward the Jordan River. They scramble to escape this suddenly hostile land and return to the Midian Desert.

Now is not the time for celebration. There is work to be done. Every survivor will someday pose another threat. Israel must pursue the fleeing enemy and not allow them to regroup. Gideon sends for reinforcements. Remember those 22,000 and 9,700 who were sent home? Now is their turn to join the fun. There is no reason for them to be afraid. The hard work is done. The three hundred selected warriors have served God's purpose—to cause the enemy to destroy itself. It is time to mop up. They are to chase the remnants of the army of Midian and finish the job.

The men of Ephraim are given a special assignment. Cut off the Midian retreat at the shallow crossing of the Jordan River. They do a magnificent job capturing and executing two Midianite commanders, Oreb and Zeeb.

What lessons can we learn from this unique war?

First, there is no formula for fighting God's battles. Just look at a few examples from Scripture. There was the battle the Hebrews fought against the Amalekites, won while Moses stood above the battlefield and held up his staff. When his arms tired and the staff dropped, the Amalekites gained advantage. Aaron and Hur held up Moses' hands until victory was assured. There is no record of this approach in any other battle (see Exodus 17:8–13).

We all know the story of the battle of Jericho. Joshua was told to march around the city for seven days, after which the walls collapsed, and Israel's army charged in and wiped out the city (see Joshua 6:1–27). That strategy was never repeated. The next battle was won with trickery—the soldiers of Ai were drawn into an ambush (see Joshua 8:1–25). On another occasion, Joshua defeated five kings and their armies when God rained hail on them, then had the sun sit still until the Israelite army finished the job (see Joshua 10:10–14).

God loves to surprise us—and His enemies—with a host of creative battle plans. It is best if we allow Him to establish the strategy for our battles today.

Second, we must meticulously follow God's directions. Gideon might think he needed thousands of men to defeat Midian. God said He would choose the team, and in His plan, three hundred was sufficient. How Gideon deployed those three hundred—maybe he could be creative. As long as he remembered that God would do the fighting. Over and over, we see that God's people are given explicit instructions. We ignore them at our own peril.

Third, do not minimize the ability of the enemy to destroy itself. God may initiate confusion in their ranks. In many situations the aggressors destroy themselves. We saw Iran and Iraq practically destroy each other in the 1980s—hundreds of thousands died in the conflict with no resolution. Then we saw Communism implode in Eastern Europe and the Soviet Union.

The West also should be aware of how it is destroying itself. How long can a nation survive when it is polarized by political groups at opposite extremes? That should provide a cautionary tale for the people of God. Today it seems as if Christians are fighting each other more than the devil. The Church divided breaks God's heart and is impotent in spiritual warfare.

Listen to the apostle Paul:

For consider your calling, brothers: not many of you were wise according to worldly standards, not many were powerful, not many were of noble birth. But God chose what is foolish in the world to shame the wise; God chose what is weak in the world to shame the strong; God chose what is low and despised in the world, even things that are not, to bring to nothing things that are, so that no human being might boast in the presence of God.

1 Corinthians 1:26–29

For Reflection

Do you agree that Christians fight each other more than the devil? Is there anything you can do to heal divisions in your own congregation or Christian community?

Secrets of God's Warriors

It would take too long to recount the stories of the faith of Gideon and Barak and Samson and Jephthah and David and Samuel and all the other prophets. These people all trusted God and as a result won battles, overthrew kingdoms, ruled their people well, and received what God had promised them.

Hebrews 11:32–33 TLB

Some were made strong again after they had been weak or sick. Others were given great power in battle; they made whole armies turn and run away.

Hebrews 11:34 TLB

After Gideon departed the scene, Israel quickly forgot Yahweh, the one who had rescued them from their enemies. They suffered from amnesia. By now they had many stories of God's saving acts on their behalf. Their Sabbath days would be ideal times to sit around the dining table or campfires and listen to elders tell these stories to the younger generation. They might also have pulled out their Bibles and studied the writings of Moses.

It was no accident that after the death of leaders like Joshua and Deborah and Gideon, within about forty years of their great victories, they slipped back into worship of idols and bondage to enemy powers. The five Old Testament warriors we have studied faced the same kinds of problems we face. The people they led were fickle and cowardly. Yet God loved them just as He loves us. God called these warriors and said, "I want to use you." His plan has not changed in three thousand years. God wants to use us!

The problem today is that we prefer solutions we can see. We put great stock in a political savior who will right all the wrongs of a nation. Charles Colson, former special assistant to President Richard Nixon, was known by associates to say that the Kingdom of God will never arrive on Air Force One.[1]

We are too easily enamored by the pomp and power of nations that it is easy to forget how fragile and temporary they really are. Sure, a charismatic leader can make a difference—in the short term. But he or she can never change hearts. As soon as the leader departs, the old problems return since the root causes have not been addressed. Our political, cultural and intellectual leaders do not recognize that there is a hidden, spiritual enemy who constantly sows discord, lies and confusion. We who are citizens of God's Kingdom are His tools to counter the agenda of this enemy.

Spiritual warfare is raging around the globe. There is an enemy who wants to destroy the Church, the Body of Christ. The dramatic increase in persecution of Christians is the most striking evidence—one in six Christians worldwide suffer from violence or severe discrimination because they choose to follow Jesus. Much of the world is closed off from traditional missionary work because of political and religious restrictions.[2]

That is why we need spiritual warriors, men and women who will reveal the spiritual power of Christ and the Holy Spirit, who will bear witness to the truth of the Gospel, who will take on the assignments God gives that will confront politics and culture and the spiritual forces of wickedness that run rampant in our age. When we respond to God's call, people will take notice and, as in the early Church, invite us "to make a defense to anyone who asks you for a reason for the hope that is in you" (1 Peter 3:15). It is not a formula for rapid change. It *is* the road to victory.

What made our five Old Testament warriors different was that they had a real relationship with God. They dared to ask Him questions about the problems in their society. They longed for God to act and asked hard questions such as "Lord, where are all the miracles?" "Why do You allow suffering?" "Where are the blessings?" Their strength was their willingness to seek out the truth and then act on it. With Gideon, it began in his home and local community, and then God used him in a wider context.

Centuries later, Jesus commissioned His disciples to spread the Gospel and make disciples, starting at home, in Jerusalem. If we cannot declare the truth at home, we will have little success in a foreign setting.

We desperately need heroes of the faith like Gideon, Moses, David and Elijah. Yes, and Jonah, too, but without his attitude. We need to be willing to discover why the people of God are being oppressed by the enemy on every front. God needs men and women who are willing to ask the right questions, and then act on God's truth. Let none of us say we cannot do these things. Whatever God calls you to do, you *can* do. There is no need to be afraid. God will give you the confidence you need to step out and take action.

The Lord wants nothing more than to involve us in His plans. He has battles for us to fight, mountains for us to climb, exploits for us to perform. He waits for us to respond to this call of Jesus: "Follow me." Our task: to share the love of God with people who are hostages of Satan in a world under his control. To be sure, we cannot hope to carry any of this out by our own power or in our own authority.

The victories of our five warriors were not won with the power of a mighty army. Nor will we win any victories this way. Rather, God delivers His people with a small band of dedicated warriors led by men and women in search of truth and who are willing to act without fear in the power that comes with obedience.

For Reflection

Are you ready to heed God's call to action? Will you do whatever He asks you to do?

Epilogue

Before you close this book, let me encourage you to take a few minutes and identify both what God has called you to do and what your battle plan is. Here are a few questions you might consider. Take some time to write down your answers.

1. What are the key thoughts you gained from these devotionals on David, Elijah, Jonah, Moses and Gideon?
2. Have you sensed a call from God to engage in a specific spiritual battle?
3. What is the first (or next) step you need to take as you follow the direction of God's Holy Spirit?

And remember, do not enter the arena of spiritual conflict alone. You need encouragement. You need others who will join you in the battle or who will back you up with prayer support.

Now, expect God to use you!

If you wish to dive deeper into the content of this book with others, go to www.aljanssen.com for a free downloadable Bible study.

And, we would love to hear how God has used the teaching of Brother Andrew in your life. You may share your stories at www.aljanssen.com.

Acknowledgments

First, I want to thank my dear friend Brother Andrew for twenty-plus years of wonderful adventures and many hours of stimulating conversation. It has been a privilege to work with your outlines, notes, sermon recordings and hours of interviews to create this resource.

Thank you to the ministry of Open Doors International, especially Johan Companjen, the founding president, for bringing me on board to work with Brother Andrew, the ministry's founder. Thank you to my friend Kurt Bruner, COO of Open Doors International, for working with me to keep the founder's vision alive.

Thank you, Sealy Yates. You are far more than an agent. You introduced me to Brother Andrew and the ministry of Open Doors International and recruited me for the USA board at an

Angels game. Your love and passion for the Persecuted Church is contagious. I am so grateful for your friendship.

Thank you to the team at Chosen Books, especially Kim Bangs, Deirdre Close, Natasha Sperling and Lori Janke.

Finally, a special thanks to my wife, Jo, who managed our home for weeks at a time while I was traveling the world and working with Brother Andrew.

Notes

Part One Elijah: 2. Ready to Pay the Price

1. According to 2022 World Watch List, more than 360 million Christians suffer high levels of persecution for following Jesus.

2. "Facial Technology in India and Its Privacy Scare," Tsaaro.com, February 14, 2022, https://tsaaro.com/blogs/facial-recognition-technology-in-india-and-its-privacy-scare.

3. John Burger, "Iraq's Christian Community Might Dwindle to 23,000 by 2024, Agency Says," Aleteia.org, July 8, 2020, https://aleteia.org/2020/07/08/iraqs-christian-community-might-dwindle-to-23000-by-2024-agency-says/.

Part One Elijah: 4. Training for Battle

1. Ailish Lalor, "The Hunger Winter: The Dutch Famine of 1944–1945," DutchReview.com, February 10, 2022, https://dutchreview.com/culture/the-hunger-winter-the-dutch-famine-of-1944-45/.

Part One Jonah: 3. Why God Sent a Storm

1. Taras Shevchenko, "In Captivity I Count the Days and Nights" (1845), trans. Michael M. Naydan, Taras-Shevchenko.Storinka.org, 2015, https://taras-shevchenko.storinka.org/taras-shevchenko-poem-in-captivity-I-count-the-days-and-nights-translated-by-michael-m-naydan.html.

Part One Jonah: 5. Time to Pray

1. "Exclusive Footage of Shahbaz Bhatti's Interview," made available by Al Jazeera, March 2, 2011, YouTube video, https://www.youtube.com/watch?v=oBTBqUJomRE.

Part One Gideon: 4. So Many Questions

1. This quote likely came from the many interactions Brother Andrew had with Mr. Grubb during Andrew's time as a student attending WEC school in Scotland.

Part Two Introduction

1. Dietrich Bonhoeffer, "Overcoming Fear," PoliticalTheology.com, August 16, 2012, https://politicaltheology.com/overcoming-fear-sermon-dietrich-bonhoeffer/.

Part Two David: 2. David Responds

1. To learn more about the Persecuted Church and how you can be involved, visit OpenDoors.org.

Part Two David: 6. Am I Ready to Fight?

1. Corrie ten Boom was Andrew's friend, and she told him that story.

Part Two Jonah: 6. A Very Long Wait

1. Abraham Lincoln, "Abraham Lincoln Quotes," GoodReads.com, accessed October 21, 2022, https://www.goodreads.com/author/quotes/229.Abraham_Lincoln.

Part Two Gideon: 1. Call to Arms

1. Milton Jones, *10 Second Sermons* (London: Darton, Longman and Todd Ltd., 2011), 54.

Part Two Gideon: 2. Who Is on the Team?

1. Nik Ripken and Barry Stricker, *Ten Big Lies about Missions* (unpublished manuscript, June 8, 2006).

Part Two Gideon: 6. Secrets of God's Warriors

1. John Stonestreet and Roberto Rivera, "Recovering the Lost Virtue of Patience," Stream.org, January 23, 2021, https://stream.org/recovering-the-lost-virtue-of-patience/.

2. For the latest research on persecution of Christians, see the World Watch List at https://www.opendoors.org/en-US/persecution/countries/.

In 1955, a young Dutch missionary attended a worldwide communist youth congress in Poland. There he discovered a remnant of the Body of Christ behind the Iron Curtain desperately in need of Bibles. **Brother Andrew** (as he would later be known around the world) distributed a suitcase full of Christian literature, marking the humble beginnings of Open Doors, a ministry to the Persecuted Church.

Brother Andrew's autobiography, *God's Smuggler,* has sold more than ten million copies and has been translated into more than forty languages. It details dangerous border crossings, KGB pursuits, and his courageous journey toward living radically for Jesus Christ.

In the early 1990s, Brother Andrew was knighted by Queen Beatrix of the Netherlands. In 1997, he was the recipient of the World Evangelical Fellowship's Religious Liberty Award, recognizing his lifetime of service to the Persecuted Church and passion for spreading the Gospel.

Brother Andrew's work through Open Doors has led the organization into places where most Christians are unwilling to go. His friendships and the love of God took Brother Andrew into private meetings with Yasser Arafat and with leaders of Hamas, Islamic Jihad, the Taliban and Hezbollah. He was among few Western leaders to regularly go to these groups as an ambassador for Christ.

Brother Andrew finished his earthly race on September 27, 2022. He is survived by his five children and eleven grandchildren, all of whom live in the Netherlands.

For twenty years, **Al Janssen** worked with the founder of Open Doors, Brother Andrew. Together they traveled to some of the places where it is the most dangerous to be a Christian. They encouraged followers of Jesus in Islamic contexts, advocating for them with government authorities and appealing to Islamic extremists while sharing the Gospel.

Using his experience as a writer and editor, Al collaborated with Brother Andrew on two major books: *Light Force: A Stirring Account of the Church Caught in the Middle East Crossfire* and *Secret Believers: What Happens When Muslims Believe in Christ.* He is currently working with Brother Andrew's papers and sermons to capture the founder's timeless messages.

Al has more than fifty years of experience as a writer, speaker and teacher. He has ministered in more than 35 countries, preaching and teaching at conferences, retreats and supporter events. He speaks on marriage, prayer, spiritual formation, leadership and evangelism and tells many stories of how God is working in the Persecuted Church.

In 2010, Al was ordained by an Anglican Bishop in an Islamic country. He retired from full-time work with Open

Doors in 2019 but continues to serve the ministry as Writer in Residence. He is an associate pastor of Holy Trinity Anglican Church in Colorado Springs where he lives with his wife, Jo, and near their three children and five grandchildren.

More from
Brother Andrew and Al Janssen

In the midst of never-ending debates, protests, riots, suicide bombings, and broken peace initiatives, Brother Andrew urged church leaders not to flee the violence but to stay and become a force for change. Through dramatic true stories, *Light Force* dives into gripping accounts of Christians caught in the crossfire.

Light Force

In this incredible and eye-opening book, Brother Andrew exposes the true stories of Muslims in the Middle East who have come to Christ and their daily struggle to survive in an oppressive land. You will be inspired by the lives of these courageous believers as well as find four practical initiatives to help your persecuted brothers and sisters.

Secret Believers

For thirty-five years, Brother Andrew's life story as a Dutch factory worker going undercover to take Bibles behind closed borders has inspired millions to step out on their own journeys of faith. His near-incredible adventures testify of God's step-by-step guidance and hour-by-hour provision—available to all who follow His call.

God's Smuggler

a division of Baker Publishing Group

Stay up to date on your favorite books and authors with our free e-newsletters. Sign up today at chosenbooks.com.

 facebook.com/chosenbooks

 @chosen_books